Strike or hartal at Chittagong.

FRAGMENTS FROM

Munewata Press, Cummington, MA 01026

2000
BANGLADESH

on the Brink of Civil War

INSIDE A COMING EXPLOSION

by Paul Ryder Ryan

ISBN 0-9662707-6-2

Also by the Author:

China Daily: Between the Lines
Copyright @ 1995
ISBN 0-9662707-3-8

Khmer Rouge End Game
(Novel)
Copyright @ 1998
ISBN 0-9662707-4-6

Published by Munewata Press
PO Box 130
Cummington, MA 01026

Cover design and text formatting by Jim Sadler

Printed by Van Volumes Ltd., 65 Springfield Street,
Three Rivers, MA 01080

Library of Congress Control Number: 00-090381

Foreword

T his is an account of my six-month quest as a Knight Fellow into the Muslim world of Bangladesh, a tiny country bursting with 126 million people on the sub-continent in South Asia. It was written as this tortured beggar nation, formerly East Pakistan, was wracked by widespread political violence, extreme poverty, economic and social disorder, an arsenic poisoned drinking water supply, excessive crime, endemic corruption, chronic power woes, and devastating seasonal flooding and cyclones. Added to these troubles was the specter of nuclear war in the region between arch-rivals India and Pakistan over disputed Kashmir.

Bangladeshis are a fiercely proud poetic people who rely heavily on the kindness of Western donor nations. My mission was to help support a free and independent press in this land still struggling to maintain a semblance of democracy that came following a War of Liberation against

Pakistan in 1971. Since that time, Bangladesh has experienced two presidential assassinations, three military coups, and nineteen failed military coups.

My entrance into the country came almost a year to the day following a statement by Osama bin Laden: "To kill Americans and their allies, both civil and military, is an individual duty of every Muslim who is able, in any country where this is possible" until American armies, "shattered and broken winged, depart from all the lands of Islam."
— Feb. 23, 1998.

I had been advised prior to departure for Bangladesh that Bin Laden agents were active in the country and that police had arrested several in November of 1988 for distributing leaflets related to the terrorist's cause.

Discussions, travels, and observations in 1999 in Bangladesh led me to the conclusion that the country is headed inexorably for a bloody civil war in the not too distant future. The necessary conditions exist for such a conflict, as this journal bears witness. Such a conflict would most likely draw India and Pakistan, long at odds over Kashmir, once more into the fray.

The Knight International Press Fellowship Program is administered by the International Center for Journalists in Washington, D.C.

Paul Ryder Ryan,
Knight Fellow, 1999,
Bangladesh

For Nayeem, Azfar, and Mukur,
who will be drawn into any tragic
civil war in Bangladesh.

And, as always, for my children—
Polly, Beth, Tad, and Michael.
And my grandchildren—
Liane and Jonathan.

"Bangladesh is like a blind man searching for a black cat in a dark room"
–Azfar, former zealot turned pundit, musician, and philosopher.

Table of Contents

Hostage to Hartal

Dhaka, Bangladesh

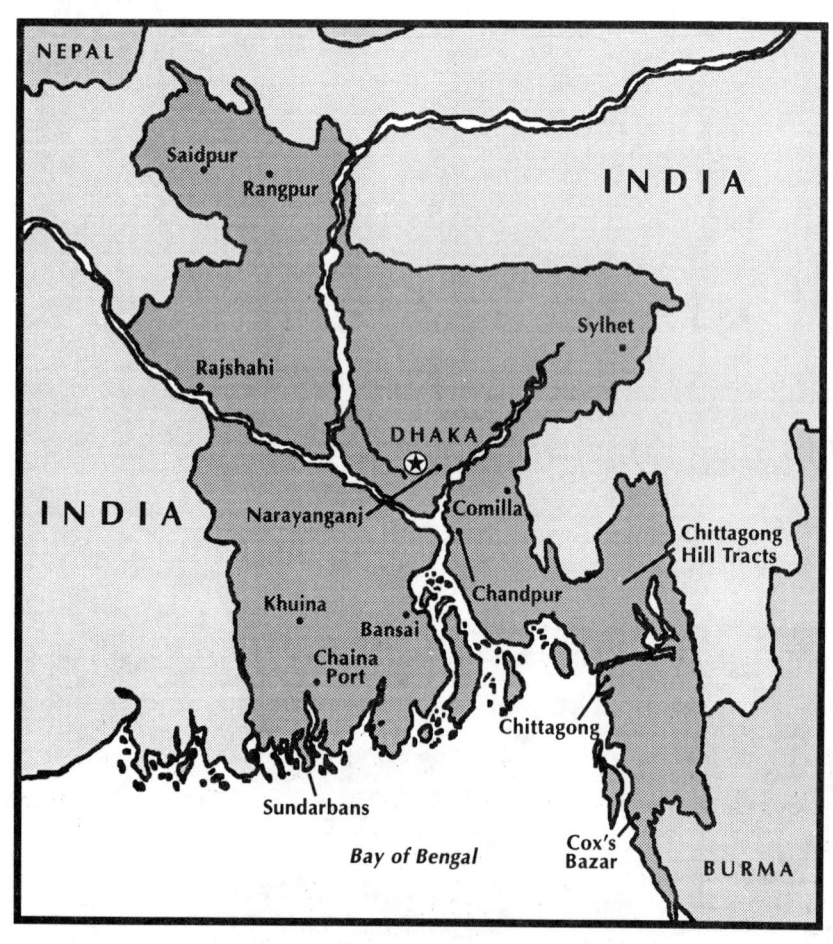

Map of Bangladesh

21/2/99

$\mathcal{A}$ rrival in suffocatingly hot Dhaka, the capital of Bangladesh, from Bangkok uneventful despite it being The National Day of Mourning for students killed in 1952's Language Movement, a critical moment on the country's path to independence. Met at the bustling airport by Hasibur Rahman (Mukur), self-described as the Administrative Man of the Bangladesh Centre for Development, Journalism and Communication. Also met by Shamshul Haque, front desk manager of the Comfort Inn, a small, modest guest house compound protected by barbed wire topped walls in the Gulshan embassy district of the city.

I must admit to being somewhat nervous. I'm carrying $13,000 in cash, $8,000 of which is a grant to the Centre from the Knight International Press Program at the International Center for

Journalists in Washington, DC. I have been directed to hand it over in two increments to Nayeemul Islam Khan, director of my host Centre. Before leaving the United States, I could find no one who could tell me the political persuasion—pro-government or opposition— of Mr. Khan. Thus, I had no clue as to whether I was being used as a conduit for funds possibly aimed at bringing down the government, gripped as it is by crippling hartals, violent street strikes that only a little more than a week before my arrival had left at least six dead and nearly a thousand injured.

Nayeem sent an old car whose make I could not distinguish around to fetch me for a buffet dinner prepared by his lovely wife at his house down a narrow alley in the heart of the city. The guest of honor was Abdul Hannan, director of the Prime Minister's Office for Culture and Communications, a career diplomat who, he said, served for some time in Moscow. Handsome with a dark mustache, he was dressed elegantly in a white tunic. His wife was bubbly for a Muslim woman. In addition, there was Farid Hossain, a correspondent for the Associated Press, his wife, and two trainers from the Thomson Foundation in Britain, presently conducting a workshop on reporting on crime, something described in my Lonely Planet guide book as almost non-existent in the country.

Abdul expressed confidence during dinner that the opposition would not bring down the government of Sheikh Hasina Wajed, head of the Awami League party and elected Prime Minister in 1996. And, at worst, there would be a caretaker government anyway until the end of her five-year term. But I came away from the meal with the sense that no one really knew what would happen in the next few days as more hartals took their toll on life in this impoverished country. The hartals coincide with municipal elections and are designed to deter

2

would be voters by providing an atmosphere of fear and intimidation.

The evening ended with a spirited discussion in some detail of the merits of Pakistan's win over India in cricket. After dinner drinks were offered all round and I earlier had washed down the delicious beef and lamb curry with a Heineken. Praise be to Allah! I had been prepared for total abstinence.

22/2/99

The big event of this sunny day was a trip by "baby" taxi or motorized rickshaw to the Green Road offices of the Bangladesh Centre for Development, Journalism and Communication. It was a wild ride in congested traffic with several near misses and a few actual small collisions along the 12-kilometer route. I barely fit in the tiny back seat of this pollution creating, but colorfully decorated vehicle. My impressions of the ride include clouds of dust, many construction sites along the way, numerous beggars, including young girls perhaps seven or eight years old at corner stops, and frequent piles of street garbage with associated black crows. Occasional white BMW diplomatic flagged cars pushed conspicuously past us adding to the horn cacophony.

The offices of BCDJC are on the second floor at 187 Green Road, actually a small alley off the main drag. The offices consist of four relatively small but clean rooms on the second floor with associated computers, and a training/seminar room on the third floor capable of handling 16 participants comfortably and 20 or so in a pinch. The room is equipped with overhead projector and whiteboards in place of the old fashioned blacks. It is a clean well-lighted place, as Hemingway might have said. From 4 pm on, the wailing prayers from the nearby mosque infiltrate the non-government Centre.

I offered a small Congregationalist prayer myself that the money ($4,000 first installment) I was about to turn over to the Centre's work on behalf of the Knight Foundation was not going to buy bullets for the opposition. But my first private meeting with Nayeemul Islam Khan, the Centre's Director, almost set my mind at ease. An intense man who had just turned 40, he explained to me in precise but halting English that he was formerly editor of two different ostensibly independent, but in reality, pro-government newspapers. He failed to mention, however, that this was at a time under the rule of Khaleda Zia, now the leader of the Bangladesh Nationalist Party, the main opposition at the moment. Nayeem assured me that the Centre was neutral when it came to politics and enjoyed support from all sides of the political spectrum. He painted himself as a man with a somewhat tumultuous past that has resulted in a lot of important contacts and who is maintaining a low profile at the moment. while attempting to raise the standards of Bangladeshi journalism. He described his first wife as a world-class militant feminist, some of whose radical views he found excessive at times, but acceptable at others. He is now married to a student half his age who hails from Chittagong, the country's main port city, and who is apparently a not too distant cousin.

We also discussed somewhat vaguely my mission at the Centre. I am to develop program training materials and workshops for newspaper science, cultural, and sports coverage. I will begin by touring government research facilities as well as university journalism departments and meeting the players. Lectures to faculty and students will be arranged. The plan calls for me to travel occasionally to several other cities and areas in rural Bangladesh, starting probably with

4

Chittagong.

Three days of nationwide hartals begin at 6 am tomorrow. Polling, meanwhile, starts at 8 am. No one seems to know quite what to expect. I will be left to my own devices during this period as travel to and from the Centre is not advised. However, travel in the Gulshan embassy district where my guest house is located is theoretically okay and I plan short trips to USIS, The Asia Foundation, and the US Embassy.

23/2/99

The Daily Star, a respected English-language daily here, reported pre-hartal violence at several sites in downtown Dhaka last night, including bus torchings, gunfire, and random bombings. "Several people, including journalists, were hurt. The casualties included a *Daily Star* Photographer who was trampled by several people in their frantic bid to escape the violence...," the paper reported. Media Watch reported attacks on journalists in the last hartal on February 10. Dhaka Medical College and several city clinics reported treating bombing victims, according to the paper.

* * *

Abdul Hannan, mentioned earlier, has an opinion piece on the editorial page of today's Star. It is critical of the treatment received by an official Bangladeshi 81-member delegation, including the prime minister, to the recent Calcutta Book Fair.

* * *

There has been no coverage, as far as I can tell, of events in Bangladesh by CNN or the BBC on its Asian programs.

*   *   *

Nayeem calls me at 3 pm and informs me he has heard there is already one dead from hartal. It could get nasty, he thinks, later on tonight and tomorrow. I inform him that I have come down with diarrhea. That was quick! He advises me not to drink the water and to be even careful about bottled water. I dip into my supply of anti-diarrhea pills obtained through the travel clinic at Hillcrest Medical Center in Pittsfield, MA, where I got a host of pre-departure shots.

My room is spartan. The mattress is hard and lumpy. There is only one heavily shrouded and barred window which faces on the back barbed-wire topped wall at the rear of the inn compound. My only wall decoration is a rather large electric clock—perhaps to remind me that check out will come sooner than I think. My closet cabinet is smaller than a coffin. The only other piece of furniture is a tiny wooden desk that doubles as dining/dressing table. My two large suitcases lie open on the floor. I do have a small TV which can get the BBC and CNN, plus a few English language movie channels. There is one local channel but I have not seen any hartal coverage. However, there have been shots of long orderly lines of mostly women in colorful saris at the polling stations. My shower though is large and could accommodate several people at one time and there is, thank God, a western toilet. A small empty mini-bar rounds out the luxury appointments. The Comfort Inn here is not affiliated with the chain in the United States.

The price of the room though is about half that paid by Paul Salopek, the former Knight Fellow to Bangladesh in 1996, for his room downtown and I'm hoping that after hartal I can rent an old tank of a car by the month that will give me the mobility and freedom to get safely about town on my own. Life is full of trade-offs.

24/2/99

The Daily Star this morning is reporting two dead and "scores" injured from the first full day of nationwide hartal yesterday. Polling for municipal elections went off relatively smoothly, the paper indicated, although there were scattered clashes throughout the city of Dhaka and elsewhere in the country. The Dhaka Medical College reported treating upward of 50 injured. "Bombs were hurled on processions, streets, buses, and other vehicles in the city," the Star reported in an abbreviated 12-page edition, normally 16.

I appear to be the only guest at the moment at the Comfort Inn. As near as I can tell, the staff consists of the front desk manager, two male room attendants, a cook, and two or three outside security guards. The Inn manager, Tony Rasheed, whom I had all my dealings with prior to coming to Bangladesh via e-mail, has yet to show his face, presumably due to hartal. Thus, I have not been able to get e-mail access yet. The fixed daily menu of the Inn has continental, Bangladeshi, and Chinese dishes to choose from.

I debated going out today and trying to make the nearby American Mission Club by rickshaw. But in the end I felt somewhat shamefully that discretion was the better part of valor given the unknown hartal situation outside and my ignorance of the language. The Star reported that most municipal offices, banks, and shops were closed in the city. Perhaps the American Mission Club was as well.

25/2/99

The second day of nationwide hartal and polling passed relatively "peacefully" yesterday, English-language newspapers (*The Daily Star, The Independent,* and *The Observer*) reported, with three deaths resulting from scattered violence that caused in excess of 100 injured, including seven photo journalists. At least 40 of those injured were termed in serious condition. Most of the casualties were victims of bomb blasts and gunfire. The Jatiya (National) Press Club in Dhaka was damaged by a bomb blast. By newspaper count, there are now five dead and more than a thousand injured, including 13 or more journalists.

The opposition parties claimed that the voter turnout at polling stations was about 10 percent of those eligible to cast ballots. It said the pro-government controlled media was giving a distorted view of what was actually happening in the country by covering only selected police secured polling sites.

26/2/99

The three-day hartal is over. However, today is a nationwide religious holiday. And most local life is still at a standstill. I can hear the cheerful sounds of children once again. They must be coming from a school courtyard next door to my Inn. The papers are reporting a relatively peaceful last day of voting with a turnout of about 60 percent. However, the opposition is holding to its position that the government figures and media coverage have been "stage managed" and that the actual turnout was less than 10 percent. It is calling for an annulment of the election results and for the government to step down.

I calculate the death toll from this hartal, judging from newspaper reports, to be at least seven dead and probably more than a thousand injured nationwide. Among the injured were at least 13 Dhaka journalists and the random violence included an activist bomb attack on the National Press Club, plus the sacking of newspaper offices.

I was struck by a rather poignant poetic op-ed piece at the top of the editorial page of today's *Daily Star* by AZM Obaidullah Khan entitled **"Do I Dare!"** What follows is an abridged and slightly edited version:

A nightmare visits me and revisits.
A city of graves is expanding its acreage.
Clouds stop moving and the shadows pause.
Trees stop breathing.
They are dying as well.

I wake up and the fear persists
like my own shadow.
Do I dare to go out?
Do I dare?
No, I am a prisoner in the solitary cell
of my house.
So is the mother next door

and the children and the neighborhood
and beyond.
They say it is for our sake,
for the sake of our rights.
For the children to grow up free
and, for me, an old man,
to die in freedom.

A distant thunder rumbles.
Stale wind smells of gunpowder
and shredded bombs. Lightning strikes,
sharp and swift like an executioner's knife.
Asphalt fumes with a bluish signal of charcoal.
The day dies and the mourners begin.
Night waits outside the door to come in
and the firefly strikes matches
Then, the smoke burns into a larger question,
one that forms and uniforms,
till the question returns.

Is it a good place to live and die in?

At the intersection, near the traffic light,
I see the crouching child.
She is selling flowers.
She begs me to buy
and I see the smudges of resignation
around her cool eyes.
Or is that fatigue?

She is tired, she is thirsty.
At nightfall she goes back to her mother,
sweaty and exhausted.
Mother lights up and pounces on her.
How Much? How much have you brought?
Listless, the child hands over the soiled purse.
She has no time to pour her a glass of water.
The child dozes off.

Fireflies strike matches.
Darkness fumes and burns.
The city of graves expands its acreage
and the question returns.

Is it a good place to live and die in?

27/2/99

Post-hartal violence continues in the countryside with newspaper reports of another two activists shot dead in a gangland-style shooting during a political headquarters card game. The toll of hartal injuries continues to mount, also. Meanwhile, rumors are circulating that an additional day or two of hartal may be called for March 1 and 2. What with religious holidays (today ís another) and hartal, the country has effectively shut down for five straight days.

My efforts at the moment are concentrated on drafting a model for a Science & Technology Coverage Workshop, settling on a monthly rental car for transportation, and setting up e-mail communications from my hotel room, which may require me to purchase an external modem for my computer. I have not seen Nayeem since last Tuesday. However, we have a meeting set for later today.

"Baby" taxied down to the Centre. Nayeem explained a three-year pilot program he is about to launch with the aim of training rural journalists. The program will begin in earnest March 9 at a police "station" about two hours from Dhaka. A "station" is really what we would call a precinct. It is a geographical area. Nayeem grew up in this particular "station" which is predominantly a rice, potato, and jute growing area. He has selected 21 journalists to participate in this program which hopes to measure the social impact on the community of the reporters' coverage. The journalists will not be paid for their participation in the program and will receive only prestige as wages.

Once the program is under way and training commences (for which I have been enlisted to help), Nayeem plans to place the journalists with Dhaka newspapers as stringers. Again, there is no pay involved for this privilege.

Following my meeting with Nayeem, I was taken to the Dhaka University Book Fair where I purchased a book on Contemporary Bengali Writers at the university press booth. On leaving the university campus grounds, I witnessed a policeman brutally beat a peanut vendor at the gate with his baton and scatter his nuts about. An ugly crowd quickly grew in defense of the vendor and other armed police arrived with rifles and automatic weapons.

We went from the fair to the British Mission to participate in a graduation ceremony for the Thomson Foundation trainers' Workshop on Reporting on Crime. The Consul handed out certificates and several other British officials were on hand. Then, I was taxied to a shop to buy a pair of shower clogs but the foot size stops at 9 here and I take an 11. The evening ended at Nayeem's place for a late buffet dinner and then I shared a car back to my Inn with the Thomson trainers who were scheduled to depart for London sometime after midnight.

28/2/99

This was a day of small victories and my first trip to The Asia Foundation, where I found a book that should prove useful in my science writing workshop. Nayeem walked away with about 20 books for the Centre's growing library. Victory # 1: My computer with the aid of a new external modem has been configured so that I now have access to both Internet and AOL e-mail: all from my hotel room (I'm reachable at rapprr@aol.com and pryan@bol-online.com. Victory # 2: A deal has been struck for a rental car and driver, which will arrive tomorrow and give me much needed mobility to get about town. Victory # 3: I begin Bangla lessons tomorrow at the Centre and should be fluent by the end of the week, barring any new hartals.

1/3/99

Today is the first day of the Second D-8 Islamic Summit meeting at the Sheraton Conference Center in downtown Dhaka. Security is very tight. No foreign visas are being issued at the moment and people seeking them are being turned down and away at the airport. You had to have them in advance for this period or you are out of luck. The D-8 Islamic countries consist of Bangladesh, Malaysia, Iran, Turkey,

Pakistan, Egypt, Indonesia, and Nigeria. Four heads of state—Sheikh Hasina of Bangladesh, Sulleyman Demirel of Turkey, Mahathir Mohammad of Malaysia and Nawar Sharif of Pakistan—are in attendance, plus high officials from the other states. The D-8 nations represent some 800 million people in the developing world. The main focus of the summit is on economic problems and fostering increased trade among member states although the D-8 members are geographically diverse and do not represent a trading bloc as such.

The summit has produced some large traffic jams in downtown Dhaka. I sat in one myself today for an hour and a half in front of the Prime Minister's residence. Fortunately, I was in my new air-conditioned Toyota rental car. My driver, John, has a beard as white as my own. It too needs a trim.

Nayeem presented me with a "wish list" of 10 programs that he would like me to participate in while I'm here. Most are workshops of four or five days duration and several will be conducted outside Dhaka. They range from workshops on basic reporting to more advanced seminars on science coverage. There are also some one-day university lectures scattered about. My task now is to flesh out the content of these workshops and to draft a calendar of precise dates when they might occur.

Shortly before coming to Bangladesh, in the course of my research, I came across an AP story about a Bangladeshi writer being forced into exile in Sweden by death threats from Islamic fundamentalists for alleged blasphemy. It turns out the writer is Nayeem's first wife, Taslima Nasrin.

I meet tomorrow with John Kincannon, the director of the USIS office here.

2/3/99

My car and driver failed to show on time because of a traffic jam downtown in front of the Prime Minister's residence. I took a baby taxi to my appointment with John Kincannon at USIS but the driver didn't have a clue as to how to find the agency which is located on the west side of one of the best graveyards in Dhaka. The building itself is the former residence of a prominent Bangladeshi involved in the War for Independence.

John Kincannon, a large pleasant Minnesotan with a beard, who has been on assignment here for about two years, professed no knowledge of the Knight Foundation and started the conversation by drawing me out on this subject. So, our talk began with a lie.

Kincannon said that he had been impressed with the quality of Nayeem's final report at the end of his USIS-sponsored recent trip to the United States to learn how to document Human Rights abuses against journalists. Nayeem visited the Committee to Protect Journalists in New York and the Sloan Kettering Institute for Public Policy in Dayton, Ohio.

The USIS officer and occasional Deputy Chief of Mission indicated he was prepared to financially assist some of Nayeem's projects, including possibly a couple of my workshops.

In response to my question, he said he put no credence in reports that Bangladesh was producing parts for India's and Pakistan's nuclear programs. He said Bangladesh had one old nuclear reactor but that it had been shut down a couple of years back and that he doubted the government was stripping the parts and delivering them abroad.

Kincannon did say that the US was interested in the prospects for

Bangladeshi natural gas development. He said the US government believed that the Bangladeshis were proceeding in this area with a great deal of flawed data and information. I later broached the idea of a seminar for journalists on this subject with Nayeem and he was receptive.

When I broached the subject of the US position vis-a-vis the present government here and the opposition, Kincannon declined to comment. Another US official source, however, later portrayed the leaders on both sides as "dictators." And said both sides were "control freaks." The source pointed out that Prime Minister Sheikh Hasina when out of power had called some 170 hartals, although she now professes they seriously disrupt the economy. Both sides are cut from the same cloth. If they changed sides, the source philosophized, you wouldn't notice any foreign policy difference.

The recent US dissatisfaction with Dhaka's shrimp exports to the US also came up for discussion. Apparently the US claims the exports were of an inferior class and passed off as being top quality. However, inspection controls have been implemented and the situation is improving, according to Kincannon. One of my environmental courses will use the shrimp industry as a case study.

The meeting between Kincannon and myself ended with his sponsorship of my application for membership in the American Mission Club.

Later, Nayeem and his wife drove with me to the National Martyrs' Monument about an hour and a half outside Dhaka. It was a dirt road most of the way choked with dust, buses and trucks. We arrived just as they were closing the gates, but talked our way in for a quick look see in the dark. The monument was one of the ceremonial sites where the D-8 ministers laid wreaths during their two-day stay.

The ride out and back afforded me the opportunity to have a long one-on-one discussion with Nayeem about journalism in Bangladesh in general. Among the things I learned, for example, is that the taking of money from sources by reporters as payment for writing favorable stories is a common practice. The average wage scale for senior reporters is about 7,000 taka per month ($140).

Then, I was surprised to learn that the AP and Reuters bureaus here are entirely staffed by Bangladeshi journalists, which might account for the sparse hartal coverage and the accompanying street violence, which is still continuing around the country with daily reported killings of political leaders on both sides of the fence.

One of the papers Nayeem worked for in the past was *The Independent*, apparently about six years back. The Prime Minister then was Khaleda Zia, now the leader of the opposition Bangladesh Nationalist Party (BNP).

Bangladeshis eat late. We ended up at an Indian restaurant near my guest house at 11 pm. We were joined by one of the Directors of the BCDJC, a woman who is also a professor of journalism at Rajshahi University where I will give lectures, and her husband, Registrar of the private North-South University with an enrollment of about 15,000. I think this university may be the only private one in Bangladesh. The mutton dish was wonderful. I arrived back at the guest house well after midnight. My day had begun at 4:30 am

3/3/99

A British photojournalist, Mike Herd, and his camera crew, working for the American Discovery Channel, came under armed attack by "hoodlums" in late February while on location filming royal bengal tigers in the Sundarbans, *The Daily Star* reported. According to Herd, a Scotsman, his vessel was boarded and his life threatened at gunpoint after he protested the dumping of garbage into the nearby mangrove waters by an adjacent speedboat. One of Herd's crew was reported to have been severely beaten. The Prime Minister earlier in February had declared the Sundarbans, long a wildlife sanctuary, a World Heritage site. There are believed to be somewhere between 350 to 450 Royal Bengal Tigers left in this country, many in the Sundarbans, an area of extensive mangrove forest.

✳   ✳   ✳

The D-8 Summit has concluded with a Dhaka Declaration pledging greater cooperation among member states. The next summit will be held in Cairo in 2001.

✳   ✳   ✳

Met with the people at Reuters. Anis Ahmed is the bureau chief and he reports to Singapore and thence to London. Formerly, he was under the direction of the New Delhi office.

Met with Nayeem. The schedule is firming up for my training courses and it looks like I will be very busy from here on in. Bangla lessons may finally begin day after tomorrow.

Dinner at the American Mission Club. Downed a small "Phillie" sandwich with a Fosters. Can't wait to get in the pool and get a little exercise.

4/3/99

In the absence of a local barber, I went to the Sheraton, which just a day before had seen security soldiers for the D8 Summit in jungle camouflage outfits toting AK 47s in the lobby, and treated myself to a haircut and beard trim. $5.

*　　*　　*

More pieces to add to the Nayeem mosaic. It seems he was married three times, not twice, the second knot being a brief interlude after his divorce from Taslima Nasrin, the militant feminist now in exile in Sweden. His current wife's name is Namma Khan Monti.

*　　*　　*

I learned a little more about the root differences between the ruling Awami League (AL) and the Bangladesh Nationalist Party (BNP). While philosophically their positions are about the same on major economic issues, the AL has historical ties to Bangla nationalism and the 1971 Language Movement which is rooted in West Bengal or Indian culture and thus is more tolerant of Hinduism. The BNP, on the other hand, has historical ties to Pakistan and thinks of itself as the champion of Bangladeshi nationalism. It is this ethnic difference that explains much of the present violence between these two political factions.

*　　*　　*

It appears traveling on the roads in Bangladesh is far more danger-ous than hartal Yesterday 10 people were killed and 75 injured in three separate road accidents.

*　　*　　*

The European Union, an important development player here, issued a statement yesterday expressing "serious concern" about the country's deteriorating political situation which, it added, is making effective cooperation increasingly difficult. Hartals and other forms of violent political confrontation endanger the lives and well being of innocent citizens, disrupt public life and inflict serious losses upon the economy which has not yet fully recovered from the effects of the catastrophic floods of 1998," the German statement issued on behalf of the EU stated. The EU, however, reaffirmed its commitment to help relieve poverty in Bangladesh.

5/3/99

Here's a thought for today. If you moved all the people in the world– more than 6 billion– to the United States, the population density in America would still be less than that in Bangladesh, which is about the size of Wisconsin with about 126 million people. There are 2,255 people per square mile here.

✳ ✳ ✳

Started Bangla lessons today. My teacher's name is Rupa and she had a dot (tip) in the middle of her forehead. Is she ever a knockout, wow! She is an instructor at the Dhaka Language Institute. I'm told she also is a poet in her own right and a close friend of Nayeem. I can now say hello, goodbye, and thank you. I plan to have an hour and a half of lessons each day when not committed to a training workshop.

✳ ✳ ✳

Added two new words to my daily vocabulary—miscreants and dacoits. A miscreant is a doer of evil or an Infidel. It is a term the newspapers use here for troublemaker or anarchist. A dacoit is a high-status criminal who in days of yore use to serve notice on his victims that he was coming to rob them. Today they are mostly just armed thieves and burglars.

Nayeem acted as a tour guide for myself and Meirion Edwards, a Thomson Foundation broadcasting consultant. We visited a Hindu mosque and two other Muslim mosques, including the National mosque which has some 60,000 people offering prayers on occasion, although the average daily turnout is about 5,000. The West Cummington Congregationalist Sunday turnout of about 30 souls pales by comparison.

I took Meirion, a Welshman, to dinner at the American Mission Club. A nice chap, he is married with four children back in Britain. At the end of his mission here, he flies to Yugoslavia for training sessions there and thence back to Laos and Cambodia for the Indochina Media Memorial Foundation. The IMMF, based in Bangkok, was my host organization on my last Knight Fellowship.

6/3/99

A story out of Cox's Bazar today says drugs, arms, and cigarettes are being smuggled into Bangladesh from Burma in salt bags. Meanwhile, an upsurge in political violence has been reported in nearby Chittagong, the major port city in Bangladesh and one of the places I am scheduled to give a workshop. "Everyday is marked by killings, gunfire, and even journalists are not spared by the terrorists. Killings and gun-battles have become a regular feature of life in Chittagong," *The Independent* reported.

* * *

Another piece added to the Nayeem mosaic: *The New Nation*, another daily English-language newspaper here, today carries a one column picture of Nurul Islam Khan and underneath it the headline reads **"Death Anniversary of former MPA Nurul Islam Khan."** The text of the story follows:

"The first anniversary of death of late Nurul Islam Khan, former member of the East Pakistan Provincial Assembly, will be observed today (Saturday), says a press release.

"Late Nurul Islam Khan, the youngest son of late Dr. Amanat Khan of Debidwar thana under Comilla district, died of a sudden heart attack in Comilla on March 7, 1998, at the age of 64. A noted lawyer, late Khan was also the Deputy Leader of the Opposition in the erstwhile East Pakistan Provincial Assembly in 1965.

"It may be mentioned that Nurul Islam Khan is the father of four sons and two daughters, including journalist Nayeemul Islam Khan, Executive Director of Bangladesh Centre for Development, Journalism, and Communication (BCDJC).

"In observance of the day, various religious rites, including Quran khawani, milad mahfil and munajats will be held in Dhaka, Comilla town, village home of late Khan and Debidwar thana sadar today (Saturday.)"

*　　*　　*

Nayeem confessed with a sigh that living in Dhaka is becoming more difficult with each passing day. His apartment has no running water as is the case with many other apartments in the city. He must arrange to truck bottled water in until the crisis passes. His wife has arrived at the office, which still has water, to take a shower.

Nayeem is closing a deal today for new office space "in the best part of town." He hopes to be in the new office by June and will continue to rent and use his Green Road space so the organization can expand. The other office has parking space along with it that will allow for holding large Centre conferences. It is also written in his lease that he may enjoy the fruit trees in the small garden that comes with the office while the landlord is visiting America.

My Bangla teacher today taught me how to say "I love you." Is there any more to learn?

Tomorrow I'm off with Nayeem to Comilla in Debidwar thana, about 90 klicks outside Dhaka.

7/3/99

When Nayeem says the trip is a two hour drive, you can safely double the time it takes to get there. It was a long day over perilous roads in the thick of dust. I left the Comfort Inn at 7:30 am and returned choked and wheezing from the dust and nursing the beginnings of a cold from the air conditioned car a little after 9 pm. Nayeem, his wife, and myself made the pilgrimage to Comilla in Debidwar ostensibly to check on arrangements for our March 11 talk to some 21 or more rural journalists aimed at urging them to participate in Nayeem's three-year pilot program that would measure the effects of newspaper coverage on the community.

A huge blue banner was strung across the entrance to Debidwar, which, Nayeem said, announced my coming on March 11. Debidwar is the market town for nearby farmers who toil to bring in rice, jute, and potatoes from their fields.

It also was a day of cemetery visits. The first was to a cemetery for British RAF flyers who lost their lives in World War II combat near here fighting the Japanese. Then, we visited the village of Nayeem's family where he offered a prayer with the local Imam (priest) in the

23

village cemetery for his late father. On the way, our car was stopped by a crowd in the road hovering about a dead body that had been recently hit by a passing vehicle. A member of the crowd asked Nayeem for a contribution to the funeral. He gave and we were allowed to pass on.

The village of his father, Nayeem said, had some 12,000 to 14,000 inhabitants, but I only saw about a dozen. We left the main road and traveled some distance over a narrow rutted dirt road that could easily have been mistaken for a path. At the village, there were tin roofed houses with cement walls; goats and cows grazed about; lush green rice paddies soaked up the broiling sun; fetid ponds hosted ducks and bathing children; I was offered coconut juice from the nearby palm trees and a sweet; everyone was most courteous.

On the way back to Dhaka, we visited a couple of archaeological sites in Comilla that date back to the fifth century. One was the remains of a Buddhist monastery and the other a site that once housed a large Buddha, now apparently residing elsewhere. There are no funds apparently for upkeep of the sites, although a small museum is adjacent to the sites with a modest collection of artifacts. We also passed the plush grounds of a high school which Nayeem attended. I learned that he holds a BA and Masters in communications from Dhaka University. Then, we visited the grounds of a large UN Development Complex and took tea just off the large library. Nearby rural people are brought in and trained in good development practices.

8/3/99

Two bomb blasts about five minutes apart at an open air concert last night in Jessore near the Indian border left eight dead and more than

150 injured, among them several in critical condition, according to the local newspapers. Organizers of the event blamed Muslim fundamentalist terrorists. The police arrested five persons in connection with the blasts, which they said they were the work of highly trained bomb experts.

Prime Minister Sheikh Hasina, meanwhile, said her government had information to the effect that the opposition BNP had formed ten terrorist goon squads with the purpose of conducting disruptive activities at public functions.

In other news, the police in Chittagong rounded up some 170 people in an effort to restore a measure of law and order there. Nayeem today announced that we will be traveling to Chittagong next week for a workshop and not Rajshahi University as previously planned.

My Bangla lessons are going well. I can now say "you are very beautiful." Rupa comes from Sylhet, tea and orange grove country.

I am consumed by the overwhelming feeling that the country could explode at any moment. It is a tinder box waiting for the right spark.

9/3/99

Another long day. Up at 5 am for a 6:30 start to an all-day seminar in Debidwar on the basics of rural journalism, but my driver fails to show because of a faulty car and it is 10 am before another car can be found to take Nayeem and myself. It is a three and a half hour drive one-way over roads that are more hazardous than a battlefield. I have learned that it is the rare driver in Bangladesh that actually possesses a driver's license. Fortunately, the car is new and the air con in good working order.

Passing through the relatively prosperous town of Comilla on the way to Debidwar, we pass a small college where entrance exams are in progress. Small groups of men surround candidates outside the gates and Nayeem explains that they are selling crib sheet answers to the test. A prime example of the corruption in the education system. Apparently cheating on exams is so widespread that Dhaka students often travel to the countryside to take their entrance exams, thus guaranteeing admittance.

The seminar is held in a large auditorium and there are banners up all over town proclaiming me to be a Media Messiah from the great state of Democracy in America. Praise be to Allah! The advance publicity has drawn 36 or so wannabe journalists. My mission is to sell them on signing up for a week long workshop in May to be held in Dhaka. I give about a two hour talk covering the highpoints of basic journalism and a few of the lower ones, too. I also try to convey the notion that journalism is an honorable and old profession that can have a positive and beneficial affect on their community. My talk seems to be well received and there is a long question and answer session following my remarks. Nayeem, meanwhile, speaks for about three hours in Bangla describing what they can expect from participating in his three-year pilot program aimed at strengthening rural journalism coverage.

I was struck by the fact that the majority of those in attendance were lecturers from a nearby university. Among them were lecturers in Physics, Chemistry, English and Economics. I had expected farmers or people more closely tied to the soil.

Before handing out certificates of attendance that bore the ICFJ and

BCDJC logos, we took a leg stretch in the form of a two column one mile walk through town with Nayeem and myself in the lead of the banner-bearing procession. It was very hot. I shamelessly dropped out about half way and trailed the procession in our air con car.

During the drive back to Dhaka, still on the theme of honorable old professions, I learned that prostitution is alive and well in the capital and that the Gulshan Embassy district where I am quartered is also the number one red light district. The number of cat houses is considerable, according to Nayeem, and they are frequented by Bangladeshis and foreigners alike. One can apparently contract the ladies by the hour, day, or for longer periods. "This is a well kept secret in our Muslim society," Nayeem commented. He went on to say that prostitution did not exist in the countryside because men were able to take pretty much whomever they liked at their pleasure and that rape was common. In response to my obvious question, he said the incidence of AIDS was thought to be very low in Bangladesh with only about 50 confirmed cases reported, but that the figure in all likelihood was nearer 5,000—still small compared to the population of 126 million and the large number of cases reported in India and Pakistan.

It was near 10 pm when I arrived home in the heart of the Red Light district and I was too tired to make a night of it despite having packed an ample supply of viagra. Dreams of winged Chittagongs danced in my head.

10/3/99

A meeting in Paris today of donor nations expressed deep concern about the continuing political intolerance and violence in Bangladesh.

The nations included Australia, Canada, Denmark, France, Germany, Italy, Japan, the Netherlands, Norway, Sweden, Switzerland, Britain, and the United States, plus the Asian Development Bank, the European Commission, and World Bank. The US has donated some $500 million in the last two years to Bangladesh and there is more than a billion dollars in aid still in the pipeline. This, is, of course, a country that literally survives off the kindness of donors.

The statement read in part: "Bangladesh's development partners are deeply disturbed by the increasing political confrontation and polarization that is jeopardizing prospects for for the country's economic growth and development. Political instability in Bangladesh is inflicting a serious cost on the nation. It has slowed down the economy, disrupted the flow of Bangladesh exports, and prevented Bangladeshis from earning a livelihood for their families and themselves. It exacerbates law and order problems. It discourages domestic and foreign investors. The real challenge to Bangladesh is the elimination of poverty..."

The statement called for all sides to resolve political differences peacefully in Parliament. Fat chance, I think. Democracy is in peril here. The violence is an endemic part of the culture and thus the political system. It gives people something to do in the insufferable heat. It is a primal instinct, a substitute, if you will, for more carnal desires.

The opposition, meanwhile, has called for a day of protest on March 13 for what they term indiscriminate arrests of their leaders and activists across the country. In Parliament, the BNP members staged a stormy walkout when they were denied the opportunity to discuss the Jessore bomb blasts.

Meanwhile, the spirit of Butch Cassidy and the Sundance Kid is alive and well in Bangladesh. At least 30 people were injured when an armed gang of "Dacoits"(robbers) last night entered passenger compartments on the non-stop express train between Dhaka and Chittagong. A number of passengers were beaten and stabbed as they were being relieved of their personal possessions, particularly cash and jewelry. Women were not spared. The band of Dacoits apparently boarded the train in Dhaka and stopped it before reaching Chittagong, where the gang made off with the loot. On reaching the train, police arrested six suspects—all crew members.

. . .Another Bangla lesson. I am learning my vowels and how to count.

11/3/99

Had my first car accident today on the way to the office. A foot long gash was put in the rear door of my white Toyota on the driver's side where I was sitting by a new bronze Toyota at a roundabout. Whip lash. I was studying Bangla at the time and was taken by surprise. A police officer told us to move out of the circle but that was the end of his concern. After about a five-minute argument in the street with a host of rickshaw drivers looking on, my driver collected the business card of the other driver and that was that. I believe my driver was not at fault as we were struck on the side from the rear.

My beautiful Bangla teacher with long black hair to below her waist is married to a doctor and has a baby son. *Quel damage!*

Thursday is pizza night at the American Mission Club. Not bad.

12/3/99

The Home Minister, Rafiqul Islam, responsible for law and order in Bangladesh, has been replaced by Mohammad Nasim in the wake of widespread violence in the country, particularly in Jessore, Rushdia, and Chittagong. Sheikh Hasina made the critical cabinet change yesterday.

Mukur, the Centre's Administrative Man who has confided in me to a dark 15-year political past in the wilderness of commerce, says Rafiqul was "an honest man," and that Nasim has a large army of terrorists of his own. If this is true, things just might get worse before they get better.

The other big story of the day is the beginning of a Test cricket match today between "Asian giants" Sri Lanka and Pakistan in Bangabandhu Stadium in downtown Dhaka.

The first rain shower since my arrival occurred today and cooled things off a bit.

Friday here is the equivalent of Sunday in the United States. It is a day for Muslim prayers and attendance at mosques. In the morning, the roads are blessedly free of heavy traffic. Banks, government offices, and many businesses are closed today and tomorrow.

Power outages are becoming more frequent and the area where the Centre is has no public water. It has to be bought by the truckload and pumped in to a holding tank, then boiled and filtered.

13/3/99

Took the day off to prepare lesson plans, read, and relax. Had dinner

with two nice English ladies who have arrived here at the Inn to interview the elderly for fund raising efforts back in the UK.

14/3/99

After a morning touring the National Museum and a Bangla lesson, I
was headed to a concert of santoor music (100-stringed ancient Indian
instrument similar to the hammer-dulcimer in America) when the car
suddenly ran into an "agitation." It was something similar to a tornado. Nayeem and I were in the back seat talking when all of a sudden
the rickshaws in front us turned about and swept past us in the oppo-
site direction like a swarm of locusts. The street before us emptied and
in the distance we could see police firing tear gas at the crowds on
foot up ahead. We quickly told the driver to put the car in reverse and
then after a bit turned it around and fled with the mob. Nayeem said
the area up ahead had been one of educational institutions and industrial organizations. We had probably run into a student demonstration
that had gotten out of hand.

The "agitation" had interrupted an interesting conversation about
Nayeem's two top aides—Azfar Aziz and Hasibur Rahman (Mukur).
Both it seems were former members of the pro-Moscow faction of the
Communist Party here who served as armed cadre. Both are close
long-time (since high school) friends of Nayeem. When the Soviet
Union went down, the leaders of the Moscow faction of the
Communist Party here pushed their cadre into the market sea and
told them to sink or swim. Nayeem, who I suspect was either in the

31

party or a sympathizer at one time, has hauled them aboard the Centre's good ship Democracy outward bound to the future of Bangladesh. What we have here is the paling of ideology from a bright red to a pink elephant in the democratic sense—a small cell of osmotic, disillusioned former pro-Moscow militant Communist cadre looking to board the "better world" train.

Azfar, the pleasant Marxist-Leninist poet, musician, and folk singer, who once led cadre rallies with stirring marching songs, confided in me that he had spent two years in Libya, ostensibly working for the multinational Esso conglomerate on its pipeline operation. Both Azfar, who just came aboard at the Centre last month, and Mukur now are married with children to support. It will be Azfar the Humorless who will accompany me to Chittagong this week as my guide/interpreter cum bodyguard.

Meanwhile, Nayeem confided that another Bangladeshi friend had flown in from London the day before yesterday to do an investigative report for the BBC on the killings at the open air concert in Jessore mentioned earlier. This source who has now returned to Dhaka is convinced the bomb blasts were not the work of Muslim fundamentalists, but the result of a dispute within the Communist Party there. The party had been the sponsor of the concert. The dispute, he thinks, may have been between the former pro-moscow faction and the hardcore center which now takes its lead from China. Nayeem says there are many former pro-Moscow Communists still adrift in the political flotsam of Bangladesh. The death toll at Jessore has risen to 10 from 8. Some 150 were injured in the blasts.

✳   ✳   ✳

The spirit of the Mafian Godfather is alive and well in this city. *The*

Independent has an exclusive story today saying that 30 heavily armed terrorist gangs rule Dhaka's underworld. The story quoted a source within the Criminal Investigation Department of the Dhaka Metropolitan Police. Gang members are seldom arrested much less prosecuted, the story said, because they are protected by politicians and other influential people. These gangs thrive on the drug trade, trafficking in women and children, bank robberies, extortion, black-mail, and killings for a price. The gang members are armed with sub-machine guns, AK 47s, and a variety of handguns of both local and foreign make. These gangs have political patrons and often carry out terrorist activities for them both inside and outside Dhaka. Some of the gangs are part of international networks.

*   *   *

The "agitation" did not keep me from the Santoor concert by Pandit Shiv Kumar Sharma given at the National Museum Auditorium, although I took my seat one minute before the concert was to start. I thoroughly enjoyed it but thought the music a bit repetitive for my taste. The Santoor musical instrument has its origin in Kashmir and the music is improvised much like jazz and was accompanied on this occasion by the drums of Shafaat Ahmed Khan, who served as the rhythm section. I rounded out the evening with dinner at Spaghetti Jazz, a joint up in Gulshan. You take the A(ssalmuilycum) train.

15/3/99

There are three main roads you can take to reach the BCDJC offices from my guest house in Gulshan. One of these roads is off limits to foreigners, according to Nayeem, for "national security" reasons. "It is sort of silly," Nayeem commented, "because our national security interests are well known to foreign intelligence agencies and there are published reports in this area available to any one who would seek them out." The Bangladesh intelligence community consists of the Criminal Investigative Department of the Metropolitan Police, the largely CIA-trained Bangladesh Security Intelligence (BSI), and intelligence units of the Army, Air Force, and Navy, which have a central command unit. The quality of the information collected is said to be good.

* * *

Another Bangla lesson.

Met with Khandaker Ali Asraf, editor of the weekly Onnesha, who will be my co-trainer and interpreter, for Nayeem's workshop on rural journalism.

Dinner at the home of Zafrin Z. Chowdhury, a journalism professor at Rajshahi University, where I will lecture in future. Her husband is registrar at North-South University in Dhaka, the only private university in the country. A Bangladeshi PhD student in forestry at the University of Alberta in Canada was present and I was reminded of just how obnoxious these strange creatures can be. It seems he had a bad experience with the US Immigration Department over his wife's application for a transit visa. This has produced a great deal of bitterness on his part toward Americans. Fortunately, my hosts did not have any boxing gloves in the house, although this young Turk would have been willing to go bare knuckle.

16/3/99

Met with Shafigur Rahman, the head of the Journalism Department at
Chittagong University, to discuss my program there. My opening lec-
ture to students and faculty will be entitled "Democracy and the
Media." It's all Greek to me

17/3/99

Today is a national holiday, the birthday of the Father of the Nation,
Bangabandhu Sheikh Mujibur Rahman, assassinated in 1975. He
would have been 79 today. Bangabandhu is credited with freeing the
motherland from the iron grip of Pakistan after having suffered
extreme persecution himself.

*   *   *

Met with Mahfuz Ullah, Secretary General of the Centre for
Sustainable Development. He is a very sharp and knowledgeable individual who will be my co-trainer for the Science Workshops, which will
focus on case history studies of the arsenic problem, hybrid crops,
shrimp culture, and oil and gas development.

Nayeem described Mahfuz as "the best journalism trainer in the
country."

He has worked in China as an expert for the Foreign Language
Press and is fond of things, if not "part," Chinese (Paul Salopek
described him as a closet Maoist). He quizzed me extensively about
my time in China (two years). In addition to his considerable newspaper experience, he also has worked (1984-85) for the Bangladesh gov-

ernment as a press officer in its Calcutta legation and alluded to recruiting a journalist spy network there. Judging from his comments, he has traveled widely, but not to the United States, although he seems well-informed about events in America.

We discussed, in part and in a very general way, the Harkatul Jihad, the militant or terrorist wing of the Muslim fundamentalist movement here.

18/3/99

There are officially some 50,000 beggars in Dhaka. The real number may be much higher. I count them like sheep to fall asleep at night and then they appear in my dreams one by one at my car window. I have yet to give them a single taka. That is my Knightmare. When I awake, I will give them 1,000 taka each.

*　　*　　*

The papers are full of violence and death. Bombings, shootings, mobs on the rampage, road casualties and such. Students at Dhaka University damaged some 50 vehicles today in a campus protest. There is unease reported on other campuses.

*　　*　　*

Preparations have begun for the three-day Eid-ul-Azha Muslim religious holiday beginning on the 29th, also known as Bloody Eid. Muslim custom calls for the sacrifice of an animal (cow or goat) in every family and, I'm told, the roads will run red with their blood until the rain comes to wash it and the stink away. The holiday is equivalent to our Christmas and many Bangladeshis will travel to their local villages for gift giving and celebration.

Chittagong,
the Hill Tracts,
the Shanti Bahini,
and my audience
with a King

Moung Shwe Mory

Murang villagers in the hill tracts.

Marma tribal King Moung Shwe Eru Chowdhury and the author.

19/3/99

F lew to the port city of Chittagong on Biman, the Bangladesh government airline. The 45-minute Foekker 27 turbo prop flight was delayed two hours, a common occurrence I'm told. The journey from the airport to the Golden Inn where I will stay was made more eerie by a citywide power outage. We drove and dined by candlelight. Azfar, who came from Dhaka in my rental car, and I are sharing a small double room that has air con, TV, and a small fridge. What more could you ask for? A room at the rear of the hotel, as the truck horns blast away until early in the morning.

It was nice to see big sea-going tankers once again. There were several of them at dry-dock on the river on the way into Chittagong— superstructures all lit up festively from their own generators. The driver had difficulty finding the hotel in the dark and we made several wrong turns.

I later learned that the port part of the city is off-limits to foreigners and that they have to obtain a special permit to enter after surrendering their passports. I did so want to steal a super tanker. And my marijuana supply is running perilously low.

20/3/99

Drove out to Chittagong University for a chitchat with the faculty and students of the Journalism Department.prior to my opening talk tomorrow on the "Media and Democracy" which will kickoff three days of seminars. I will be introduced by the two Vice Chancellors and then the Department Chairperson.

As if I didn't have enough hazards to contend with, such as treacherous roads (my car has had another small accident; front fender bent and right signal light out), random gunfire, teargas, malaria (epidemic outbreak in Sylhet), and such, the lecturer who greeted me warned me straight away to beware of snakes, specifically cobras. Seems they have a tendency to come down the slopes into the classrooms through open windows. They are common vipers on the 1,400-acre campus set in gently rolling hills. I told him I would keep my charm poised and ready.

The gray drab cement campus buildings look tired and somewhat stained from the blistering sun and the strain of learning. The architecture looks as though it was the inspiration of a prison warden. At the entrance gate, where our car had to receive clearance, three policemen armed with rifles Kipling might have faced sat dutifully in the shade waiting for trouble. In our drive to the main faculty building, I noticed a great deal of construction under way. It turned out to be Intermural Sports Day combined with some oral exams for some students and there were no classes in progress.

Met with about 20 wannabe journalists in the student cafeteria. Tea, fruit cake, and questions. Then, a cluster photograph session outside in front of the library. Pleased to see seven or eight young women among the wannabes.

I learned the Journalism Department has two IBM computers which are theoretically supposed to be used by faculty and students, but in reality are used for administrative purposes. There is no access to the Internet.

The university, which is located 16 kilometers from the city limits and takes about an hour to reach by car from the hotel, has about 14,000 students. A shuttle train takes students back and forth and campus buses take over from there.

21/3/99

About 90 students and faculty, a near full house, turned up for my lecture on "Democracy and the Media," held in the university library's amphitheater auditorium. The university's two Vice Chancellors said a few introductory words as did the acting Journalism Department Chairperson. I talked for about an hour and then fielded some tough questions for more than a half hour (Why is the US bombing Iraq?, What do we have against Muslims and Islam?). A Chemistry professor in the first row led the heckling.

My talk seemed well received. There was a round of polite applause following my prepared remarks. The power went out a couple of times during my talk and I had to almost shout to make myself heard above the prayers being entoned over the loudspeaker outside.

On departing the auditorium, we ran into a protest procession of about 100 members of the militant wing of the Muslim Fundamentalist Movement. They were marching three abreast and shouting slogans. My entourage quickly gave way.

Nayeem did not attend my lecture. He pleaded a headache. But I think it was a fib. The local Journalists Association was having an important all-day meeting at the Press Club. Then, too, he may have been exhausted. The night before had been his first night in some time with his young wife who is a student at Chittagong University. The hotel manager, Chittagong's equivalent of Edward G. Robinson, turned Monti and Nayeem rudely away in an ugly scene, refusing them a room. Azfar suspects he thought Monti a prostitute. They were forced to seek a room at a nearby hotel.

The car died of a sick carburetor on the way back to the hotel from the university. The rest of the day was consumed arranging another vehicle. We settled on a Toyota mini-van for the same price as a car.

After my final lecture on Wednesday, Azfar and I will drive to Bandarban, near the Burma border, to spend a night with the hill tract tribes there. Just a year or so back, this area was the location of a small 22- year insurgency by tribal guerrillas known as the Shanti Bahini against the government and its efforts to resettle large numbers of Bangladeshis in the region, much the same as China did in Tibet, with the idea of them being assimilated into and dominating the tribal cultures. Even though some of the guerrillas, who numbered about 5,000, have laid down their arms, including rocket launchers, in a peace deal with the government, one still needs special permission to travel there, which we don't have. But we do have press contacts in the area. It should prove interesting.

23/3/99

My lecture today was limited to 40 students from the Journalism Department of Chittagong University, nearly half of them, I was pleased to see, women. I talked for an hour and a half about the Internet. Not one student had a computer and none had ever been online. The interest was intense and the question and answer session afterward lasted more than an hour.

After a tea break and a snack, I showed the video "Getting the Story" in a small room off the University Museum, which has a priceless collection of Buddhist stone art and artifacts.

At the tea break, the department chairperson, Tahmina Aakhter, confided to me that she would be immigrating to the US this summer with her two daughters, 8 and 5. She will be living in Queens, NY. Did I think Queens would offer a better life than Dhaka, she asked. The questions keep getting tougher and tougher.

Meanwhile, the papers tell the story of a young girl who was raped and then thrown from the roof of a four-storied building recently in Chittagong. She lay unconscious in a pool of blood for nine hours before policemen finally decided to take her to a nearby hospital. More shootings of political activists reported with one dead.

Discovered my first really good restaurant in Bangladesh since my arrival. The Hong Kong, specializing in Thai and Bengali dishes. Chittagong is a large city with a population approaching six million. I find it more pleasant and less threatening than Dhaka.

23/3/99

The roads are a cattle drive. Farmers today are driving them to market for slaughter at Eid, competing in single-lane space with rickshaws, baby taxis, trucks, cars, and our green Toyota mini-van. "It is their (the cattle's') one opportunity to go straight to heaven," Azfar comments as we stop on the way to my morning lecture to view and feed the huge turtles of the whirling dervishes. They are the size of Galapagos tortoises and tourists feed them bread in their small pond in front of a temple. If you are not careful, they will take the bread, stick, and your arm with it.

My lecture today is on "The Craft of Journalism." There are 17 students in the audience when I start, but within 10 minutes the number swells to more than 50. With question and answer time at the end, the session lasts two and a half hours. I cover the basics in Jack Webb style—"just the facts," which Norman Mailer once reminded a judge at the trial of the Chicago Seven "are nothing without their nuances." Touched a little on ethics and then felt guilty accepting gifts at the closing ceremony.

It is near 2 pm when we depart for Bandarban, an impoverished town of some 40,000 souls in hill tract country about 80 kilometers from Burma. We take along one of the journalism students, Moung Shwe Mory, who is the grandson of a tribal chief. He is a third-year student and a wannabe photo-journalist.

Along the way, we pass over the longest toll bridge in Bangladesh, which is sorely in need of repairs. It seems the government leases the toll concession to a private individual for a considerable sum who then pockets all the revenues.

After a three-hour plus ride delayed slightly by an overturned truck in the middle of the road left like a dying elephant with spinning wheels in the air, we reached Bandarban nestled in a valley on the banks of a river. The surrounding hills are the color of drought and have the smell of slash and burn cultivation practices. The local Press Club has arranged for us to stay at an isolated government guest house situated on top of a hill at about 2,000 feet above sea level. Nearby Kewkradong is the highest peak in Bangladesh at 3,172 feet. There are no other guests at our house, only a caretaker and two sleepy watchdogs. There are no restaurants as such for foreigners in Bandarban. Azfar buys some eggs to boil and some veggies and bread for a meal.

I had the foresight to buy a cheap picnic cooler back in Chittagong and we stocked it with orange juice and chicken sandwiches bought at a bakery. We also brought along a supply of bottled water. The power in Bandarban when we arrived, of course, was out. It would come on intermittently during the course of the evening. We sat for awhile in the Press Club (a converted narrow shop stall off the main street) and I answered the questions of seven members present.

Then, Moung Shwe called "the King," his grandfather, Moung Shwe Eru Chowdhury, and obtained an audience with him for us later this night. He is 82 years old and the 15th Bohmang chief of the Marma or "Mro" tribe. We hurriedly run out to buy a gift for the King, which the young Moung Shwe helped us pick out. It was a tastefully elegant sari which set me back about $6.

The Bangladesh government has appointed a new King, but the tribal people do not recognize him as their chief. Moung Shwe Eru remains their King and one of his six sons will succeed him.

"Boh" means general and "mang" chief in Burmese. The King or Raj, as he is referred to, rules over an area of 170 square miles and has 109 village headmen under his command. The Marma tribe, which settled in the area some 400 to 500 years ago from Burma, is the second largest after the Chakma of the 11 main hill tribes in the tracts.

It seems the King is the equivalent of our IRS. His main function is to collect taxes from his subjects. He also is the protector of his people in general, ombudsman in land disputes, and is dedicated to preserving the indigenous culture.

My hour and a half audience with the King takes place in his tasteful but not lavish apartment. My mind associates it with a monastery sanctuary and indeed the King is a Buddhist with monk like characteristics. His English is excellent, learned from Catholic Canadian missionaries when he was young. And his mind is very alert. We swap dragon tales and Buddhist lessons while also discussing the forces of change on ethnic minorities. The King has served several times as a Member of Parliament in various Bangladesh governments as a tribal representative.

It is after 11 pm by the time I turn in under mosquito netting, but there are not too many about at 2,000 feet. The day began at 5 am. Tomorrow the young Moung Shwe will take us to visit the villages of two different tribes and I will be the subject of a formal interview at the local Press Club.

24/3/99

The main hill tribes are thought to have settled in the tracts, which cover more than 500 square miles, in three migratory stages. The first to come from Mongolia were the Mizo, Pankhu, Mru, Khyang, Khumi, and Banjugi, followed by the Tripura and Murang, and then the Chakma, Marma, and Ryang.

We pick up the young Moung Shwe and another local tribal journalist and head for a Marma village about 16 kilometers outside of Bandarban. The village of about 250 people is relatively prosperous. For one thing, it is accessible by car. The buildings are made of wood and the roofs thatched. The women and children are very shy and back into their houses whenever I point my camera toward them, although I have been assured it is alright to take pictures. Pigs and chickens move about in the space beneath the houses which are elevated off the ground for flood season. There is one well for drinking water and a nearby river serves for bathing and cleaning purposes. The ground is baked brick hard by the intense sun. But some of the houses have their own generators and a TV antenna can be seen here and there.

We then head for a Christian Murang village high on a hill about 8 kilometers from Bandarban. Our minivan has trouble getting up to this village which requires that we pass through an army checkpoint. The last couple of hundred yards we have to trek in, a steep uphill climb. I have to be pushed much of the way and reach the top nearly dead from exertion. I will drown gasping for air in my own pool of sweat. We halted our climb half way up when a jeep loaded with heavily armed soldiers in helmets and combat gear passed slowly on the road below. There was some apprehension. They spot us, but probably decide the climb is not worth it.

The headman of the village invites us into his house, which he made himself about 10 years ago. Three women, two with small children, greet us. We are offered water from the clear running stream below.

There is a small communal church near to the headman's house. The headman, fortyish, owns about 15 acres on the top of this hill which is given over mainly to banana and pineapple growing. There are 190 people in his village of 80 families. He was trained by Catholic missionaries and on our departure takes us into the simple Church where, on rough hewn log pews, he shows us his grandmother's beautiful handicrafts. Both Azfar and I buy some.

On the path downhill, I keep a sharp eye peeled for snakes, which is about the only wildlife left in this region aside from some 20 species of birds. Twenty years ago, I'm told, the area was a haven for leopards, jackals, fox, monkeys, tigers, and deer.

It is 1 pm by the time we reach the offices of one of two daily newspapers in Bandarban. I give an hour and a half interview to the Murang journalist who has accompanied us. He has prepared questions and several other journalists from the paper hang over his shoulder as he interviews me.

I avoid a question about What do I think of the Shanti Bahini situation? It seems the government has broken several of its promises to the guerrillas which were made to get them to lay down their arms.Not all the Shanti Bahini have laid down their arms and unrest, I'm told, is brewing once again.

We leave at 2:30 pm for Cox's Bazar, Bangladesh's only seaside resort town with a reputation for harboring big time smugglers. The trade is in heroin and arms from Burma which is just a few kilometers away by boat or overland route. The trip will take about four hours.

We check into a large beachfront hotel. It has a golf course and swimming pool as well as private beach and a bar, but only a handful of guests of which only one is a foreigner. The room is nice and spacious. We attempt to eat in the large empty hotel restaurant but no food is available because they have run out of cooking gas as has their supplier. We decide to try a seafood restaurant down the road. Again, we are the only diners and this restaurant, too, is without cooking gas. So there is no supply of fish. But the manager says he can fix us some Bengali dishes. I settle on one that has prawns as the main ingredient.

The manager relates that he has had to change his menu as there has been little call for fish dishes by tourists, which have been few in number this year and last. We are visiting at the tail end of the high season.

25/3/99

Aside from a meeting at the local Press Club, the day is devoted to relaxing. It is too hot to swim in the pool. The golf club bar is closed due to a lack of customers. And there is very little activity on the beach. Besides I don't have a swim suit with me. It's enough to drive me to a Buddhist temple, the Burmese market, and a film developing shop!

26/3/99

The entire day is spent returning to Dhaka—a four-hour, bone-crushing drive over roads mostly under construction (we inch pass another overturned lorry) to Chittagong, then lunch, and a wait for a 3 pm flight which miraculously on this prayer day is not delayed. Having paid for and left the minivan in Chittagong, Azfar will travel by air-conditioned bus back to Dhaka. He has managed to purchase the last available ticket this day, but the bus will not depart until 11:30 pm. He will be glad to get back as he suffers from migraine headaches and lost his pills in Bandarban. I fear looking after me has just aggravated his condition.

Met at the airport in Dhaka by Mukur. His eyes light up when I tell him in jest I met representatives of the Shanti Bahini guerrilla movement in Bandarban. He confides that in his past he once spent 21 days with them as part of a training program.

Dinner and e-mail at the Comfort Inn followed by BBC news of the bombing in Kosovo.

27/3/99

Yesterday was Bangladesh National Day, or Independence Day, the country's 28th since the War for Liberation from Pakistan, and the papers are full of stirring songs and words about fighting for democracy and freedom. This massive assemblage of words and songs can be thought of as a dirge for martyrs.

A lead feature article in the weekend Independent magazine supplement is entitled "Freedom's Eternal Flame."

Another article in the same issue asks the question: "What is a journalist?" The answers range from Joseph Pulitzer's "primal force in society" to a Bengali writer's description of "illiterate ghost."

The author quotes Pulitzer as having written "A journalist is a lookout on the ship of state. He notes the passing sail, the little things that dot the horizon in fine weather. He reports the drifting castaway whom the ship can save. He peers through fog and storm to to give warnings of dangers ahead. He is not thinking of his wages or the profits of his owners. He is there to watch over the safety and welfare of the people who trust him."

I am reminded of the Ancient Mariner, icebergs, the Titanic, and the Wreck of the Edmond Fitzgerald.

While away in Chittagong, my lectures received a fair amount of coverage in the Dhaka press. I also was the subject of a feature article in the largest Bangla newspaper in the country, a tabloid.

*   *   *

Headlines that caught my eye on return: COUNTRY HEADING FOR WORST POWER CRISIS: SUMMER OF DISCONTENT AHEAD. DONORS WILL NOT MAKE PLEDGE AT AID CLUB MEETING:ASSISTANCE TO DEPEND ON PERFORMANCE. ONE KILLED, 20 HURT AS BLC FACTIONS TRADE SHOTS IN CHIT-TAGONG. 10 BOMBS RECOVERED FROM MP'S HOUSE IN SYL-HET. USE OF SURFACE AND RAIN WATER ADVISED TO AVERT ARSENIC PERIL. US AMBASSADOR FAVORS EXPORT OF GAS. NO GAS EXPORT NOW: HASINA. ONE SHOT DEAD, 100 SHOPS DAM-AGED IN KHULNA AS TRANSPORT WORKERS CLASH.

My Bangla lesson was cancelled because my teacher had a recording session.

Murang headman explaining village life.

Eid-ul-Azha

28/3/99

𝒯he five day Eid-ul-Azha holiday, which always coincides with a full
moon, has begun with 32 reported dead in highway accidents already
as Bangladeshi humanity crams into and on top of buses and trucks
headed for rural villages and towns. Several of the dead were killed in
Comilla and Chittagong.

Bloody Eid is actually celebrated tomorrow. One of the greatest
Muslim festivals of the year, the holiday has its origin in a tale about
the Prophet Ibrahim. He was called upon to sacrifice what was most
precious to him. After two days of offering sacrificial animals, he
learned that it was his dearest son whose sacrifice was needed. But
when the Prophet Ibrahim was about to carry out this sacrifice, Allah
placed a sacrificial animal in place of Ismail.

In Dhaka, it is hoped that the blood, entrails and other remains of thousands of sacrificial animals slaughtered on the roads will be properly covered so as to reduce the risk of environmental and health hazards. One offers prayers to Allah for his tears in the form of cleansing cloudbursts. Meanwhile, *The Daily Star* has reported that the armed hired goons of cattle market organizers have been forcing farmers and traders to bring their cattle to their bosses' markets. Five farmers were killed in one clash with goons.

Generally speaking, traders or "middle men" buy cattle from farmers well in advance of Eid, then have the farmers fatten the cattle and drive them to market, where the traders then sell them for a substantial profit.

Nayeem confides that he has spent 8,000 taka ($160) for his cow, a piece of which will arrive in Dhaka tomorrow from Comilla. This is a relatively small sum as the average paid for a cow at Eid is about 15,000 taka ($300) and they can run as high as 25,000 ($500) or more taka. One cow allows the buyer to commemorate seven people in his family. A sacrificial goat, on the other hand, is only good for one remembrance.

I am invited to Nayeem's house for Eid dinner. He has bought me a gift—a special Muslim tunic to wear at the feast. But will it fit?

29/3/99

Today is Eid. And there ain't no Santa Claus. Reports of the first tornado of the season up north on the border with India: 2 dead, many injured, and several villages destroyed.

The Eid holiday coincides with the Hajj pilgrimage to Mecca in

Saudia Arabia, a journey every devout Muslim is supposed to perform once in his or her lifetime. The wire services report that 1.7 million people from all over the world made the trip this year.

*   *   *

Bicycle-powered rickshaws are the ants of Dhaka. They can be seen crawling along everywhere. And they are very colorful (trucks, too). In fact, they are an art form in themselves. Some are decorated with bright pastoral rural mural scenes, birds, ducks, and the faces of attractive women with dots or tips in the middle of their foreheads. Others are decorated with Arabic fabrics and glass beads. The hand-painted scenes occupy the vinyl or tin backs of the rickshaws. One common figure is a winged creature with a woman's head. This figure is known as the *buraq*, which carried Mohammad on his ride from Jerusalem to heaven and back. The owner can have his rickshaw decorated by a local artist for anywhere from 150 taka ($3) to 500 taka ($10) and up. Miniature rickshaws can be found in the stores made of wood, brass, gold and silver.

*   *   *

Quiet Eid dinner at Nayeem's with a handful of his close friends. One of the guests is Christina Rozario of US CARE who is an Assistant Project Coordinator for a number of development projects. One of them puts women to work on road construction site.

Day Two: Id on Eid. The streets are near empty. Eerie. The country is crippled as much by holidays as hartals. When you add the two together, you get a man-made disaster—a proximity to the feeling of imminent chaos. Tell Heisenberg Uncertainty is more than a theory here, it's reality.

Ceiling fans do a dervish number on the mind. They creep into your subconsciousness and stir stale thoughts, circulating them in nether regions of the brain.

Azfar is giving the poetry of his body to his wife in Comilla.

Mukur, the mad Marxist, is wearing an expensive baby blue silk tunic and could be mistaken for a capitalist arms dealer or Arab royalty.

The people in the villages are drinking arsenic and loving it. They will eventually disappear like Alice down a tube well.

I wish it would snow.

My room is getting smaller. The Comfort has gone out of my paranoid Inn. All the psychotic Inmates apparently have gone home for Eid, leaving me in the thick of the curry.

Giving the finger to Colonel Sanders, there is a Southern Fried Chicken chain in Dhaka that is "lip licking good."

Billboards everywhere advertise cigarettes that only fools should buy, and computers that very few can afford.

You can never be sure of anything.

My language teacher failed to show. That was my Bangla lesson for today.

The poet in me keeps calling from the bathroom for more toilet paper.

31/3/99

Final day in Eiden. Looking for Eve in all the wrong places. Day spent planning, reading, writing, and studying. Most shops are closed, but a few catering to foreign tourists opened late in the day. I found a couple of open antique stores with some nice but expensive items from Burma. Dinner at the nearly empty American Mission Club.

1/4/99

Newspapers are back with a vengeance after a three-day Eid blackout. A total of 10 dead in political violence and 17 dead in road accidents, with 157 injured. Meanwhile, dacoities have been active as have mastans or gangsters at the cattle markets where they have been driving up beef prices by keeping traders and farmers away with bomb and gun intimidation.

Then, the opposition parties have been meeting to plot their post-Eid agitations. More confrontation and hartal are likely.

Nayeem informs me that the five-day workshop for rural journalists from Comilla and Debidwar begins tomorrow.

Monti and Nayeemul Islam Khan.

Brink of Civil War?

Azfar Aziz

2 to 6/4/99

$\mathcal{I}$ t was a busy week; long hours. Seventeen would be rural journalists attended the five-day course in basic journalism, held in the training room on the third floor of the Bangladesh Centre for Development, Journalism, and Communication in Dhaka. I lectured through an interpreter, Azfar Aziz, for the better part of four to five hours each day. I was pretty much a one-man show.

My co-trainer, Khondker Ali Ashraf, while pleasant enough, had an uncanny sense of when I was starting to run out of steam, and would act on that instinct to step outside the room for a smoke. Khondker, 62, a former Professor of Journalism at Dhaka University and columnist for a national Bangla daily, showed a good deal of disdain for the largely uneducated rural journalists. His main contribution to the course was a two-hour session on the fourth day devoted to feature writing. Despite this, the workshop, overall, I think, was a success. There were two dropouts and certificates were given to 15 students at a final awards ceremony attended by an official (political affiliation blurred—described to me as both AL and BNP) from Debidwar who left his bed in a Dhaka hospital where he was being treated for out of control diabetes to perform the last rites. I gave three small monetary prizes on behalf of the Knight Program for best written profiles.

✳ ✳ ✳

For the first time to my knowledge, the English language press this week carried stories initiated by the opposition parties to the effect that some government ministers were trying to push the country toward a civil war. At lunch with Azfar and Khondker on the final day of the course, I asked if they thought the country was on the brink of civil war. Khondker said no and did not comment further, but Azfar said yes. "Maybe not tomorrow, but within a year to three years, it is possible, in my opinion. It is relatively calm on the surface. The calm before the storm. But there are treacherous undercurrents."

He went on to say that the ingredients for civil war included extreme poverty in many parts of the countryside. In some places, villagers have to go without food or just one meager meal a day for five or six days at a stretch. Children are growing up by the thousands with no job opportunities and thus are becoming members of armed gangs bent on dacoitery and other crimes. Everywhere, there are daily reports of a breakdown in law and order. NGOs are compounding the problem by selective distribution of food aid and other misguided efforts. Meanwhile, Muslim fundamentalist factions are receiving and stockpiling arms from abroad and creating social tensions based on rigid religious philosophy, an example being attitudes toward women.

The fundamentalists, Azfar said, are none too happy that women head both the government and opposition. While the militant Islamic fundamentalists are small in number, they are in a position to exploit any Muslim uprising at the grassroots level.

Another factor is the perception that the Hindu minority in this country is becoming more vociferous and assertive in their demands.

Then, the government and the opposition are basically one and the same in terms of economic policy so that a change in government will not bring any real change in general conditions.

And corrupt police activities are another factor. There have already been cases of disgruntled mobs attacking rural police stations.

Meanwhile, armed pro-Chinese communists are aligning themselves with opposition parties, while former armed pro-Soviet communists are joining the ranks of the ruling Awami League. Then, there is the outlawed Communist Party members who have gone underground with their arms and are fomenting anarchy at the grassroots level in various parts of the country. They number between four and six million cadre.

Plus, the Shanti Bahini are restless once again. All this, Azfar explained, is a recipe for disaster, the ingredients for civil war. All it would take is the right leader; the right spark.

Later, without revealing I had talked to Azfar, I asked Nayeem, the Director of the Centre, if he thought the country was on the brink of civil war. He answered "yes" and basically agreed with Azfar's assessment. He differed only on the time-frame. Nayeem thought a civil war might be five or more years down the road. But it will come, he said.

As if to underscore these sentiments, the papers of April 7 carry a story that on the night of April 5 three were killed and some 100 people injured in Gopalganj when rival political factions there clashed.

Three other small stories tell of violent protest clashes by villagers in remote farming areas elsewhere in the country.

During the rest of my stay in Bangladesh, I put the question of whether or not Bangladesh faced a civil war in the not too distant future to people in various walks of life whose opinions I respected. The overwhelming response to this informal poll was "yes."

❋   ❋   ❋

Meanwhile, my trip to Rajshahi University, a spawning ground for leftists and communists, has been delayed for a couple of days pending approval. The local BNP has called a hartal for April 8 and for all students to support it. At the national level, the BNP has urged the student wings of its organization to be in the vanguard of agitation activity and has called for a nationwide protest against government policies on April 8.

The power and water supply in Dhaka remain intermittent. Temperatures are approaching unbearable.

7/4/99

In support of the proposition that Bangladesh is on the brink of civil war, *The Independent* of April 8 runs a story filed today's date from Jessore alleging that teenage boys in the rural southwestern region are being conscripted into outlawed communist political parties against their will, where they are then armed and trained to kill, loot, and extort.

Political parties mentioned included "the Sarbahara Party, the Purba Bangla Party, and different factional groups of other extremist parties." The activities were said to be occurring in 38 thanas under six districts, including Jessore, Jenidah, Magura, Chuadanga, Meherpur and Kushtia. The various factions are moving openly with their arms throughout the countryside in broad daylight.

The story added that if any family resisted giving up their son or sons to a group, they were being "threatened with dire consequences." If a son was given up, often a rival group would raid the villager's house and press the family to recall their boy and have him join their group.

If farmers resisted demands made by raiding youth, they were often killed on the spot.

*　　*　　*

Another Bangla lesson. They are getting more difficult and I have little time to study.

*　　*　　*

Took Nayeem and Monti to dinner at the American Mission Club. Neither had ever been before. I treated them to imported US T-bone steaks with A1 sauce, their first ever. Nayeem confessed to not being very adventurous when it came to food. He seldom strays from Bengali dishes. Even Thai food does not interest him. Monti, on the other hand, was more inquisitive. She selected the French dressing from three choices for her salad and said she liked it

8/4/99

Made a big mistake today and an ass of myself to boot. I bit on a story that Azfar fed me this morning about a chance meeting he had yesterday with a junk dealer in the dark, mysterious old city of Dhaka. The junk dealer was known to engage from time to time in the illegal sale of antiquities. During the course of their conversation, as Azfar related it, the junk dealer, having been told by Azfar of a wealthy American friend, mentioned that canisters of weapons grade uranium were also available on the black market in Dhaka.

The dealer told Azfar that a Russian ship had been forced aground by a cyclone sometime in 1995 or '96 with a cargo of uranium which had subsequently been stolen and moved to Dhaka.

A good portion of the uranium, the dealer said, had been sold for huge sums to India, Pakistan, and China, but that some still remained for sale. High-level Bangladeshi officials were alleged to be involved in these black market dealings.

I made the mistake of thinking John Kincannon of the USIS might be interested in this info and called him for an appointment. I caught him as he was about to depart for a week in Vienna, the home away from home of the USIS for conferences and briefings. John said he was very skeptical of the story, although he acknowledged a similar story had surfaced about two weeks back and that there had been a few others ("eight" in all). He allowed as how the CIA types in Dhaka hated getting these kinds of reports because it made for 60 or more pages of paperwork and endless legwork in unpleasant and dangerous places. I wished him luck with the cream puffs in Vienna and beat a hasty retreat. I came away with the feeling I had been set up, but by whom? It smacked of a test. I'm a sucker for derelict ship stories.

✳ ✳ ✳

Had another Bangla lesson.

Visited the offices of the daily *Manavzamin* (The Home Land), the first tabloid to appear in Bangladesh about a year and a half back. I met with all the top editors. The Bangla-language paper is flourishing with a circulation near 60,000. Three other tabloids have come on the market since the daily *Manavzamin*, which runs from 24 to 48 pages in full color. A full page color ad costs 250,000 taka ($5,000), while a B&W goes for 75,000 taka ($1,500). I will give a talk to the reporting staff on April 20th or thereabouts. There is an overall permanent staff of about 200 people, plus correspondents in nearly every major town across the country.

9/4/99

The opposition coalition has called for a countrywide dawn-to-dusk hartal on April 18, "the first of a new series of such actions." In addition, demonstrations will be held on April 15 and 17 which will effectively shut down the country for three to four days. The main aims of the agitation are to force the Awami League (AL) government of Sheikh Hasina to resign and to protest the deterioration of law and order, the rising costs of essential commodities, and the continuing crises in the electricity and water sectors. The hartal action was announced by the leader of the main opposition party, Sheikh Begum Khaleda Zia, who is chairperson of the Bangladesh Nationalist Party (BNP). The action was taken despite pleas from donor nations not to disrupt the economy.

✳   ✳   ✳

With the country awash in human misery, it is sometimes easy to push the apocalyptic environmental problems faced here into the dark recesses of the mind. One such particulate matter arises from the baleful billowing smoke emanating from the brick-fields surrounding Dhaka and other major cities. There are an estimated three to five thousand brick-fields around the capital alone spewing tons of toxic waste into the atmosphere. The law requires the chimneys from the brick factories to be fitted with filters and for the chimneys to be high enough to omit their smoke beyond human contact, but few brick-makers reportedly follow the law. A construction boom in Dhaka and elsewhere has increased the demand for bricks and compelled the yards to operate day and night . The result is a health hazard of siz-able proportion, not to mention the widespread destruction of local vegetation. A solution might be to replace the coal, wood, and tires burned in the furnaces with clean gas.

Meanwhile, whenever I take a shower or flush the toilet.here, I feel an enormous sense of guilt as well as loss due to the general scarcity of water.

*   *   *

Some humor: A used car lot was observed on the way to the office with a large sign that said Autoscan. Some one had altered the sign to read Autoscam.

I'm informed the local market has been out of beef for several days due to the large-scale slaughter and consumption of livestock at Eid. And so, on to button-size morsels of mutton.

*   *   *

I burned my right hand rather badly when I attempted to put out the rather large candle in my room following a power outage from 8 pm to 9 pm. The candle flame and wax spilled over onto my hand when I attempted unsuccessfully to blow it out. I've raised large blis-ters and must guard against infection.

10/4/99

It seems the Sundarbans, the vast mangrove World Heritage forest that spans parts of India and Bangladesh on the Bay of Bengal, is haven for a number of arms dealers as well as the endangered Royal Bengal Tiger and the South Asia crocodile, according to today's *Daily Star*. The article alleged that a number of corrupt Forest Department officials were involved in the trade as were students at Dhaka University. The going price of a single bullet is $1. The main transit route is through the city of Khulna, a jumping off point for entry into the forest region. The story alleged that the local police lacked "keen interest" in cracking down on the smugglers and reported 61 weapons had been confiscated in the last six months.

The forest also harbors a tribe of people called Bawali who make their living from tapping bee hives for the honey. These people are a favorite delicacy of the estimated some 450-350 Royal Bengal Tigers still left in the preserve. The tigers are said to be making a comeback in terms of numbers, while those of the forest bee people are diminishing.

* * *

Had another Bangla lesson after which Rupa said I'm "improving" despite a lack of concentrated study.

* * *

Mukur took me to his older brother who is in his third year of internship to be a pediatrician. No, I'm not pregnant. Mitul prescribed some burn ointment for my hand.

Power outages are becoming more frequent and lasting longer. There is no power most of the day in the Green Road BCDJC office area. The backup generator is kaput.

11/4/99

Angry mobs numbering in the thousands went on a rampage yesterday in the old city section of Dhaka burning vehicles and sacking the offices of the power and water authorities in protest over critical shortages. At least two were dead in the violence and anywhere from 20 to 200 injured in the melees. The police used rubber bullets and tear gas to break up the demonstrations.

*   *   *

Went to the Bangladesh Burn Center to have my hand dressed after my blisters broke during the night. I sustained rather severe burns over a good portion of my right hand. The Burn Center, the first and only one of its kind in Bangladesh, did a good job of treating me with minimal facilities. I'm on antibiotics.

Leave tomorrow by air for Rajshahi where I will give three days of lectures at the university there, returning to Dhaka on the 16th.

The Gravity
of Newton

Newton and Zafrin Z. Chowdhury

12 to 16/4/99

℧ he gravity of the overall situation in Bangladesh was accentuated by my harsh, punctuated encounters with "Newton" during my four-day visit to Rajshahi University. The lawless motions of this young Newton, an assistant professor in the Department of Mass Communications, perhaps in his late twenties, might best be described as theoretical anti-Americanism.

Newton, hiding behind a thin wisp of a mustache and an ingratiating smile, is the communist dervish of his Department with a substantial student following in awe over his mastery of theoreticism. A dropout from Soviet communism with still pro-Moscow leanings, he has now attached himself to the ruling Awami League as a campus agitator and spreader of the gospel according to Marx.

Rajshahi University is the second largest institution of higher learning in Bangladesh with from 25,000 to 27,000 students at any one time. The campus is large and shaded with many trees. Students mill about and talk of Newtonian physics while demonstrating a propensity to litter indiscriminately in an otherwise pastoral setting. The odd goat and cow graze about.

The town of Rajshahi dwells on the banks of the Ganges River waiting for it to overflow the fragile embankments. India is only six kilometers away and many people without travel documents swim back and forth on a daily basis. The town looks prosperous and reasonably clean. The narrow side-streets are crammed with bookstalls as befitting a university town.

After arrival by plane from Dhaka, Azfar and I went straight to the university where I was introduced to the faculty and acting chairperson of the Department, Zafrin Z. Chowdhury, a longtime friend of Nayeem's and a director of the BCDJC. I had been to dinner at her apartment in Dhaka a few weeks before. She informed me that I would only have two days of lectures instead of the planned three because the 14th was Bangla New Year and the university was closed. It was decided I would lecture on the Internet on the13th and on Democracy and the Media on the 15th. Did I have a copy of my talk on Democracy and could they copy it for distribution to the students so they could follow along? I did and they could. That settled, I was invited to tea in the evening at the Faculty Club. Newton smiled engagingly.

Newton and one other professor, the two who would verbally assassinate me at my final talk, were the only ones who turned up for tea at the Faculty Club. We sat formally in a room that could have held 100 people easily. Newton questioned me extensively about my early life and it was evident that he had studied my CV carefully. The game of insult and embarrassment had begun.

My lecture and question and answer session on the Internet the following day went pretty well. There were between 50 and 60 students and faculty in the audience. None had a personal PC and only two or three had ever accessed the Internet. The session lasted about two and a half hours. In the late afternoon heat, I visited the local museum which has some fine pieces of Muslim, Hindu, and Buddhist art.

On Bangla New Year, I visited Puthia, 22 kilometers distant from Rajshahi, known for its Hindu temples and old Raj-era palace. A game of cricket was in progress on the parched lawn in front of the sadly neglected structure, which is on the verge of becoming a ruin. Also visited an Ashram some seven kilometers distance, which houses what is left of a collection of Hindu art. The leader of the Ashram was forced to flee to India during recent troubles. The temperature was in excess of 105 degrees and sapped my stamina, but the real heat would come from Newton tomorrow.

My lecture on Democracy and the Media, held in a seminar room of a remote building on the large campus, started an hour late. At the scheduled starting time, 12 noon, there were three students in the audience. It was extremely hot outside and Bangla New Year processions were still in progress on the campus. By 1 pm, the number in the audience had swelled to about 40. Newton and his accomplice straggled in. My talk lasted about 45 minutes and was supposed to be followed by a student question and answer session. Instead, the podium was turned over by the chairperson to Newton who launched a long prepared diatribe (longer than my speech) against my talk and American imperialism in general. The bombing of Saddam came into it as well as Belgrade and American attitudes toward Muslims. He cited

Noam Chomsky ad nauseam as the source for his critical remarks about the American media, which, in his opinion, is "controlled" by big corporations that are largely an extension of the US government, voicing its propaganda. Newton's polemic drew applause from five or six students in the audience when he said visiting Americans always present themselves as "superior" to Bangladeshis. By the time Newton's colleague had his critical turn I was numb from the bombardment of misconceptions, lies, and half truths. Nearly two hours passed in this rebuttal before the students, those who were still left (perhaps 12 to 15), were given an opportunity to join the crucifixion.

I had been led into an unethical academic ambush.

On the return to our guest house, we passed a grandstand set up on one side of the main thoroughfare. Some 300 or more people were seated in the road listening to an orator from the People's Workers Party. Prominently displayed on the side of the bandstand was a banner with the old Hammer and Scythe symbol displayed.

A planned meeting for an interview in the evening with members of the University Press Club failed to materialize.

Power outages are common in Rajshahi.

Flew back to Dhaka on the 16th. The ride to the airport was shared with the acting chairperson of the Journalism Department within the Mass Communications Faculty. and her seven-month old daughter. I told her of my displeasure with the way I had been treated on the final day. She apologized and said the actions of the faculty were beyond her control.

In general, I felt the trip had been a waste of time and money. It certainly was my worst teaching experience in Asia to date.

✻ ✻ ✻

Meanwhile, the army was called out today (the 16th) by Prime Minister Sheikh Hasina to guard power and water supply stations from rampaging mobs in Dhaka, Chittagong, and elsewhere.

On arrival in Dhaka, I went straight to the Burn Center to have my hand redressed. I am continuing on antibiotics. The hand, although ugly to look at, does not appear to be infected at this point.

A day of nationwide protest demonstrations is scheduled for tomorrow (the 17th), followed by a countrywide dawn to dusk hartal the following day (the 18th).

17/4/99

Nayeem went to Debidwar today and won't be back until the 19th. Azfar has been left in charge of the BCDJC office which shows no sign of activity beyond my Bangla lesson. Azfar confided to me that my Bangla lessons will serve as a model for the new language section within the School of Communications that will be launched in June at the newly rented office space uptown. Azfar will be director of the School of Communications and Rupa, my instructor, will be head of the language section, which will solicit students from the visiting foreign community.

The School of Communications will offer week-long seminars in various journalism topics for 500 taka ($10) and it is hoped that I will lead a few of these workshops early on and thus be a drawing card. The seminars will be open to professionals and wannabes.

The USIS has withdrawn its promised support for a science workshop in early May led by me on Oil and Gas Development issues, according to Nayeem and Azfar. No reason given. Nayeem still plans to hold the workshop, but at a later date. Dhaka University, meanwhile, has pushed back my late April lecture dates until the middle of May, saying they were unable to find a suitable seminar room.

*   *   *

In a surprise development with possibly far-reaching consequences for the Asian sub-continent, the Indian coalition government of Prime Minister Atal Behari Vajpayee fell by one vote (270-269) today in a confidence motion in Parliament. Italian-born Sonia Gandi of the once vaunted Congress Party will attempt to form a new government, which would be India's sixth in three years. She faces resistance because of her foreign birth.

The Hindu nationalist Bharatiya Janata Party (BJP)-led government's defeat could push the world's largest democracy into a prolonged period of instability. The leadership crisis comes at a time when India has provoked an arms race with arch-rival Pakistan by recently test firing medium range missiles capable of firing nuclear warheads. Pakistan has responded by twice test firing missiles of its own.

*   *   *

Meanwhile, scattered violence continues across Bangladesh at the village level. Six persons were shot to death in two villages of Sadar thana in the District of Meherpur. The deaths appeared to be the result of a feud between two political factions. About 25 armed men were said to have participated in the raids on villagers' homes, causing widespread panic. The number of similar deaths since the beginning of the year in the region was put at 24.

80

Azfar believes a harsh hartal may be in store tomorrow. He has advised me to travel by rickshaw and not car. Some 6,000 policemen have been called out in Dhaka to maintain law and order in addition to the army units already guarding water and power sources.

18/4/99

The feeling that I have traveled back in time to my assignment here was confirmed today as the country entered the Hijri year 1420. The National Moon Sighting Committee met at the Islamic Foundation in Dhaka and set holy Ashura for April 27.

Whatever the position of the moon, the opposition let it be known that they wouldn't bet sixpence against another nationwide hartal on May 4, timed to coincide with by-elections in Meherpur. The pace of agitation is accelerating. The opposition will conduct a week of nationwide "agitations" from April 23 to 27.

In the fun city of Rajshahi, which I just visited, the opposition plans a rail/road barricade program on April 22 with the aim of disrupting traffic in the northern region and I suspect, creating mass anger.

The overall casualty total from today's hartal is reported to be at least 150 injured in sporadic clashes across the country, including about 100 in Dhaka, where crude hand-made bombs thrown at buses were a feature of the day. But the toll may be much higher because I get the sense that news coverage of the strike is being deliberately down-played in advance of an annual two-day meeting opening in Paris tomorrow of donor nations to Bangladesh. The political violence here has led some analysts to speculate that aid pledges, seen by some as a measure of faith in the current government, will be considerably reduced this year.

19/4/99

Purchased four books at the kiosk at the Pan Pacific Sonagaron Hotel, perhaps the best watering hole in town. Also bought a fruit cake from their bakery to go with my afternoon tea.

The books were on Election Reporting in Bangladesh, a 1999 Bangladesh Yearbook, published by *The Independent* and patterned after *The Far Eastern Economic Review* yearbooks, and two Bangla language for foreign idiots paperbacks.

* * *

In continuing news from Rajshahi, the Bangladesh Institute of Technology there was closed today for an indefinite period following a clash on campus Sunday between rival political activists which left 25 students injured.

* * *

In what could signal the beginning of widespread conflict at the grassroots level, an anonymous official source has told *The Independent* that the police, army, and units of the Bangladesh Rifles (BDR) will soon launch a "special combing operation" in 10 districts of the Khulna Division in the southwest in an attempt to restore law and order there. The operation will include one platoon (1,500 men) of regular army troops, plus two platoons (3,000 men) of BDR soldiers. The military units will be under the command of the district police authorities. The story quoted unofficial sources as saying that some

1,200 people have been killed in the Khulna Division by marauding politically-motivated terrorist gangs since the first of the year.

*   *   *

Meanwhile, a border skirmish between India and Bangladesh erupted this morning at the Jamalpur Border Observation Point in Daulatpur thana. Six Bangladeshis were reported killed in the skirmish and some 60 others wounded, mostly from mortar fragments.

*   *   *

Last-minute invitation for dinner at the Santoor, an upscale Indian restaurant in downtown Dhaka. Nayeem and Monti are celebrating their first wedding anniversary. Zafrin and her husband, the Registrar of North-South University, are present, as is Azfar and another couple. I present Monti with a bouquet of flowers. The food is excellent. Zafrin's husband invites me to give a lecture at his private university. He says, with a grin, he can provide three or four Newtons.

20/4/99

Had a bad power day! The Gulshan area where I reside was without electricity for five and a half hours (10 am to 3:30 pm) and the phones were down as well. Missed a Bangla lesson and an appointment with the co-trainer for my Arsenic Workshop, coming up the last week of April.

Tony, the Canadian/Bangladeshi manager of the Comfort Inn, informs me that he has moved an Indonesian spy into the room next to mine. He described himself as a "political officer," Tony confided, "and you know what that means."

Dinner at the American Mission Club. On this hot and muggy night, the Australian beer brought out the aborigine in me.

21/4/99

My Toshiba laptop computer has detected a virus. The computer's Mcfee anti-virus protection system informs me the virus is "LP EMF 0741.T" and that it cannot eliminate it through cleansing and suggests deleting the program where it appears and then reinstalling the program. This is my first experience in dealing with a computer virus. I call Henry Hilton, Mukur's friend who helped me link up with Bangladesh Online. After describing the problem, Henry says it looks like a new strain of virus most probably picked up through e-mail on the Internet. He tells me to bring the computer by and he will try to find a more up to date anti-virus system for me that can eliminate the bug. I do.

* * *

Bangla lesson.

Meeting with Mahfuz Ullah, co-trainer of my Science Writers Workshop: Focus on Arsenic Water Contamination, scheduled to begin on April 28 and run five days. Twelve mid-level (three years experience) journalists have been selected, all but one from the English-language press. They will be paid a daily per diem (150 taka each $3). Mahfuz, head of the Centre for Sustainable Development, which doubles as a clipping service, and I settle on three top-notch local guest speakers. They will be paid a modest honorarium.

22/4/99

Morning spent researching arsenic water contamination problem and Zeroxing relevant papers for hand-outs.

Bangla lesson.

Trip to bank safety deposit box.

Fresh dressing put on hand at Burn Center. It appears to be healing, but slowly. Minimal dressing allows more air for faster healing. Continuing on anti-biotics.

Mukur, the Administrative Man of BCDJC, is a member of Narcotics Anonymous, which has more than 500 members in Bangladesh. He is a leader of the organization here, which has branches worldwide. A person at the Comfort Inn who knew Mukur in his Dhaka University days described him as a brilliant student but a bad character on campus, involved in arms dealings. He seems to have straightened his life out. Heroin was his downfall. He certainly has been very friendly and helpful to me.

My computer is back in operation. Henry has eradicated the virus, hopefully, and installed an F-Secure system especially designed to protect Windows 95.

23/4/99

There is a sharp contrast between coverage of yesterday's events in *The Independent* and *The Daily Star*. The latter newspaper chose to push all stories of violence off the front page, while *The Independent* leads with the death of two people and injury of some 50 others in clashes with police at Khagrachhari in the Chittagong Hill Tracts. The Star's inside story uses the figure of 150 injured.

The clashes occurred at three different locations when police attempted to turn back tribal activists who were seeking to attend a banned anti-peace deal rally on the grounds of the Swanirbhar Bazar. The rally was organized by the Pahan Ana Parishad and the Hill Women's Federation, according to a statement by the United People's Democratic Front, a coalition representing several hill tribes in Dhaka.

The police allegedly fired on the activist tribal processions without provocation. Day-long clashes in several towns throughout the hill tracts ensued with tribal activists resorting to "cut rifles, pipe-guns, and arrows" in retaliation. Several policemen were wounded.

The United Front has launched a campaign to reject the December 2, 1997. peace agreement between the Parbatya Chattagram Jana Sanghati Samity and the government, which ended a bloody 22-year insurgency by the Shanti Bahini, a guerrilla group of about 5,000 members. The United Front maintains the government has failed to keep its promises to the tribes made under the agreement which saw the guerrillas give up a large number of their weapons.

Prime Minister Sheikh Hasina was awarded the UNESCO Peace Prize this year for having brokered the Hill Tract peace agreement.

∗   ∗   ∗

Meanwhile, in Dhaka. some 100 people were injured as opposition activists clashed with police in the busy commercial area while attempting to picket (gherao) power installations in the capital. More protests are planned for Sunday (the 25th). A number of home-made bombs were hurled during the street demonstrations in which the police responded with tear gas and rubber bullets.

In addition to seeking an uninterrupted supply of electricity and water in the city, the opposition is trying to force the government to step down, thereby paving the way for mid-term elections.

*   *   *

The Independent also carries a small Page One story alleging that the CIA used an an old World War II grass airstrip near Dhaka in 1957 for a covert operation in which they dropped two specially trained Khampur agents into Tibet to disrupt Chinese activities there. The source of the story is Newsweek magazine. The code name of the operation was St. Circus. Bangladesh was then East Pakistan and Pakistan an ally of China.

Spent day preparing for workshop on arsenic contamination of drinking water.

24/4/99

Temperatures hovering around 105 degrees F. for the last several days. Became dizzy during my Bangla lesson. Dehydration suspected. Took some salt tablets and am drinking lots of bottled water.

Met with Ainun Nishal, who will be the guest speaker on opening day of the Science Writers Workshop. He is country representative of The World Conservation Union, an engineer, and an authority on Blangladesh's water problems. He will give an overview of the state of science in this country. Seemed a genial man with a sense of humor.

Roughly 75 million people in Bangladesh are at risk from drinking water from tube wells that have excessive amounts of arsenic in them. Some years back, UNESCO prescribed digging more than four million wells as a way to curb water-borne diseases that were taking a large toll in human life at the village level. The World Bank helped finance the wells.

Death from arsenic poisoning is not pretty. It can take anywhere from eight to twenty-five years to die (depending on individual tolerance level and amount ingested) from the odorless and tasteless element, which is naturally occurring in the Earth's crust. The US EPA standard is 50 ppb or 50 micrograms per liter. Up to 10,000 micrograms per liter has been found in Bangladesh tube well water. The government here first became aware of the problem somewhere between 1990 and 1992, but moved very slowly, perhaps because Dhaka wells were not affected, in dealing with it, which means from this point on more and more exposed people at the village level will be falling fatally ill. The severe symptoms are skin cancer, kidney and liver failure, and respiratory diseases. Bangladesh's hospitals are not equipped to handle a large number of such cases.

Beard trim and hair cut at the Pan Pacific Hotel,

Hand seems to be improving, but very slowly. There is still a danger of infection.

The police today launched a countrywide crackdown on terrorists, rounding up somewhere between 1,352 and 2,000 known criminals. The action came as gunmen killed three villagers and wounded another 10 in two separate incidents in the district of Kushtia. There are 64 districts in Bangladesh.

25/4/99

Political violence continued in downtown Dhaka today and across the country as rival political factions clashed with police and each other. I was forced to take an alternate route to the offices of BCDJC after an opposition procession was broken up by a thrown hand bomb near the Prime Minister's residence. Several people were injured, including policemen, and 10 vehicles were damaged in the fray.

In Jamapur, where a half-day hartal had been called by the opposition, one person was killed and an estimated 50 others injured when rival political factions clashed. Other political violence and injuries were reported in Strajhani and Jessore.

*   *   *

Met with Dr. Mahmunder Rahman, a Trustee of the Dhaka Community Hospital. He will be the featured speaker at my Science Writers Workshop on Arsenic Contamination in Ground Water. He has been dealing with the problem for several years and is one of the few in Bangladesh who has accurate data on this crisis that affects many people, perhaps upwards of 75 million.

Power outages continue: Five of more than an hour duration in the BCDJC office area.

Met with head of Sayedpur Press Club where I will be giving a four-day workshop following the Science Writers Workshop. Sayedpur is in the northern part of the country and they say that on a clear day in October you can see the third tallest peak in the Himalayas.

Hindu temple at Puthia.

The Chernobyl Computer Virus

The author@explaining.com the Internet.

26/4/99

$\mathcal{T}$he Chernobyl or CHL computer virus struck Bangladesh with a vengeance today, shutting down thousands of computers in Dhaka and across the country. At least 3,000 computers crashed in the initial stages, according to reports by the Bangladesh Computer Society, and estimates of those infected ranged as high as 60,000, a perhaps inflated figure since others estimate the total number of computers in the country at 50,000. In addition to personal PCs, the virus hit banks, embassies, including the US , the stock exchange, commercial houses, and government offices.

The virus wipes out data on disk drives or makes it impossible to start up the computer. It is said to originate in Asia and is timed to activate on April 26, the 13th anniversary of the Chernobyl nuclear disaster. It is specifically targeted at Windows 95 and 98 and NT systems. June 26 is another activation date.

*   *   *

Meanwhile, acts of violence continued unabated. At least seven people were killed in the district of Chuadanga when some 35 armed members of the outlawed Purba Banglar Communist Party .entered a village there and removed eight people from their homes, taking them to a nearby high school before slaughtering them one by one in execution style on the school grounds.

*   *   *

The opposition coalition has promised to intensify its efforts to bring down the government.

Newspapers describe the heat as "unbearable." another in a long line of inaccurate statements, but close nevertheless. Power outages continue.

Another Bangla lesson.

Frantic preparation for Science Writers Workshop on Arsenic Water Contamination.

27/4/99

Today is a public holiday known as holy Ashura. There is no absence of things to pray for.

Azfar informs me that Nayeem is steaming having lost all the data on his home computer thanks to a rat having eaten away the connections at the back of his computer. The office computers appear to have escaped the virus attack because no one has accessed the Internet in several days.

28/4/99

Today is the first day of my workshop on Writing About Science: Focus on Arsenic Water Contamination: Twelve mid-level professional journalists on hand, including two women who work as sub-editors for local wire services. The rest are a mixture of editors and reporters with from three to five years experience on Bangla- and English-language newspapers. The session, from 9 am to 4:30 pm with lunch and tea breaks, went pretty well.

29/4/99

Day Two of workshop.

The newspapers are continuing to give Page One treatment to the Chernobyl computer virus. Latest official figures put the number of known crashed computers at 5,000 with an estimated 15,000 more infected. Computer vendors put the total number of computers in the country at 50,000, 80 percent of which are in Dhaka and 15 percent in Chittagong, with the remaining 5 percent spread out across the country.

One knowledgeable source told me he believes the figures are exaggerated and that vendors are using the scare to boost computer and motherboard sales. All statistics in Bangladesh are suspect, he said. Take population figures, he explained. They are based on some census taker asking the village headman how many live there. Usually, the numbers are vastly exaggerated in the knowledge that future aid requests may be based on his response. If you ask a farmer how far it is to his village, he will tell you 12 kilometers when it is really 2. A witness to a bus road accident will claim 200 were on board when the vehicle's maximum capacity is 50 inside and 50 on the roof. It is the Bangladeshi way.

* * *

Meanwhile, Reuters has reported that more than 8, 300 terrorists, many of them Communists, have been rounded up in police raids across the country, but particularly in districts in the southwest. The report quotes a senior police official. A relatively small number of arms also has been confiscated. Legislation allowing for summary court trials in the field is being drafted for introduction into Parliament, according to the newly appointed Home Minister Mohammad Nasim, who was speaking at a meeting of top police and government officials in Rajshahi.

The probability that the police will round up more than known terrorists in their current drive is high. A massive violation of human rights might be at hand.

* * *

Frequent recent reports of violence on various campuses around the country was highlighted today by the closure of the Bangladesh University of Engineering and Technology in Dhaka, following a series of rampage incidents sparked by the expulsion of a student. Teachers and their families and vehicles were stoned. One wag termed it "high drama." Elsewhere in the city, in the New Market area, students from Dhaka College and Imperial College clashed. The result was damage to several shops and vehicles and one student seriously injured. The clash between students of the two colleges erupted at a fast-food shop because of a perceived insult to a female student.

A Call for a Holy War

30/4/99

A possibly very significant story that would support my imminent Civil War theory (mentioned earlier) is unfolding. According to the Bangla-language daily *Ittefaq,* one of the largest in the country, on the 25th of April last in the town of Gopalganj some 50 clergymen representing militant Muslim Islamic Fundamentalists factions addressed an audience of some 50,000 followers gathered from all over the country and declared that a Taliban-style "revolution" would be launched "very soon" to restore religious principles.

Meanwhile, a police detective has disclosed that a Ukranian ship, with a cargo manifest stipulating it was carrying powdered milk, off-loaded a vast quantity of arms (a substantial number of AK47s) and ammunition that were distributed to Islamic Fundamentalist groups during the first week of April. The off-loading took place off a town south of Chittagong, a Fundamentalist stronghold. Further shipments are due and prior shipments cannot be ruled out.

A translation of the *Ittefaq* article follows: (Gopalganj is about 70 kilometers south of Dhaka.)

"Gopalganj Correspondent: A public meeting of some Muslim clergymen was held yesterday (April 25) in the local Shaheed Minar (language martyrs monument) area of the municipal park. The meeting pronounced poet Shamsur Rahman a traitor to the state. It also called for a Taliban-style revolution and to resist the conspiracy to dissolve the Madrasa (traditional, clerical) education system.

"The speakers said: 'If Allah wishes it so, a Taliban government will very soon be established in the country and the movement will start right from the very soil of Gopalganj. Today all of us here have become members of Harkatul Jihad (Holy War) at this very spot.

"Taliban members were sworn in at the meeting.

"The meeting was presided over by Abdul Mannan, Principal of Tungiparha Gowhardanga Madrasa. Hafej Mohammed Omar, one of those who ran for Prime Minister in the last general elections and the President of Khademul Islam (the Servants of Islam), was the chief speaker.

"Other featured speakers included the President of the Islami Oikya Jote (the Islamic United Front), Shaikhul Hadithí Azizul Haque, and Secretary General of the Kaomi Madrasa Education Board, Fazhul Haque Amini. Also speaking were Abdel Zabbar, Ahmadullah Ashraf, Maolana Khalilur Rahman, Ijaharul Islam, Maolana Abu Baker Siddiquee, Moslemuddin, Maolana Abu Zafar Kashemi, and Maolana Farid Ahammad.

"In all, 15 persons spoke at the gathering of some 50,000 people who traveled from different parts of the country to listen to more than six hours of speeches.

"The meeting was held in the park without the permission of municipal authorities. There was, however, a previous announcement to the effect that the rally would be held on the Bangabandhu College campus but, when permission was cancelled, the venue was shifted to the municipal park.

"The speakers demanded that the government stop oppressing Muslim clergymen and also that it release Shahidul Islam and Ahmed Shadek (a Pakistani and a South African, respectively, charged with involvement in the plot to kill poet Shamsur Rahman).

"Addressing his remarks to Prime Minister Sheikh Hasina, Abu Zafar Kashemi said that if she did not stop oppressing Muslim clergymen her fate would be more fearsome than the tragic fate of her father (who was assassinated).

"Fazul Haque Amini told the gathering that Bangladesh would be freed to establish Islamic rule. 'We are called Razakur and traitors. But, what about Shamsur Rahman, is not he a traitor?

"Shaikhul Hadith Azizul said that during the colonial era the British tried to destroy the Islamic education system and that the present government is trying to do the same thing.

"The principal enemies of Islam are now two—the present government and the NGOs.

"The principal speaker, Hafej Mohammed Omar, urged the Prime Minister to return to the fold of Islam by public 'Taoba' (formal repentance) over radio and TV."

The details of this story become vague at this point. Possibly Nayeem was contacted by someone in Gopalganj who informed him that journalists and newspapers had received death and closure threats if they reported on the event. *Ittefaq*, to my knowledge, is the only newspaper that carried the story. The other major Bangla daily, *Janakantha*, passed over the event.

Nayeem then apparently contacted the Center to Protect Journalists in New York and alerted them to the situation. He was recently recruited into the CPJ network during his USIS-sponsored tour of journalism-related centers in the US. Subsequent attempts by BCDJC staffers to confirm the death and closure threats drew denials from both newspapers and journalists.

Given the Bangladesh exaggeration factor, the attendance at the rally was probably more like 20,000 to 30,000, rather than 50,000, still a sizable number.

1/5/99

May Day: A National holiday.

The number of those arrested in the nationwide police roundup of known terrorists has swollen to more than 10, 000. A total of 151 weapons have been confiscated during the action, now in its ninth day.

Gunmen never-the-less assassinated a leading member of the Awami League party at Panba amid continuing reports of political violence around the country.

Interestingly, Reuters reports that universities across the country, including Dhaka, Chittagong, and Rashashi, were closed yesterday by a general strike led by opposition student groups. *The Independent* and *The Daily Star* did not report the action.

There is no shortage of ways to die in Bangladesh. The lead story in today's Independent reports that two more people died yesterday from sunstroke in Panba where the heat-wave shows no sign of letting up. Panba is not far from Sayedpur where I will be giving a workshop next week. The entire northern region is afflicted with severe drought, compounded by little in the way of non-contaminated drinking water and chronic power outages. Children are particularly vulnerable.

*　*　*

Talked with my farmer daughter Polly. She had to come in from spring planting to answer the phone. My grandson Jonathan is poised to take his first steps at any moment. My granddaughter Liane is doing a lot of baby sitting. Flirted with Leslie Henderson, a friend from my China days, over the Internet through AOL's instant message service.

2/5/99

Day Four of Science Writers Workshop.

*　*　*

One of my students, writing for a Bangla newspaper, quotes a forestry official as saying that in the last three years Royal Bengal Tigers have claimed more than 350 human victims in the Sundarbans.

*　*　*

In a report from Daulatdia, Reuters correspondent Nizam Ahmed writes: "Three generations of women in Marzina Begum's family have lived through history in a Bangladesh brothel.

"I don't know who is my father, my mother conceived me in this hell of a place and I have become a prostitute here," 35-year-old Marzina told Reuters in the Daulatdia red-light district, a mass of brothels that house 1,500 women and girls.

"My grandma was also here before partition of the British-ruled subcontinent in 1947 and gave birth to my mother," she said as a gentle breeze blew a stinging odor of sweat through the shacks that make up the district, which teems with women and their clients in the mid-summer heat.

"We have no family or known fathers. We are a legacy of British rule that ceased 52 years ago, but nothing has changed for us," said Laila Shipan, 25, also a third-generation Daulatdia prostitute.

"Built on the sandy shore of the river Padma in 1890, 95 kilometers (59 miles) north of Dhaka, the brothel has survived many attempts to demolish it, both during the days of former East Pakistan and in the last 28 years of Bangladesh independence.

"The hoodlums who live off the women's earnings and powerful patrons who get their sex for free — so-called "free riders" — have ensured its survival.

"We have always been backed by a strong customer interest and various groups who take a share of our income," Marzina said.

Now women's rights activists and non-governmental organizations (NGOs) try to change the lives of the Daulatdia prostitutes. Their task is not easy.

"Once a woman is identified as a prostitute, it is impossible for her to return to Bangladesh's conservative Muslim society," said Monira Sultana of NGO Save the Children Australia (SCA). She tries to give Daulatdia's girls an elementary education and to teach the prostitutes an alternative living.

"The NGOs have also taught the girls about condoms, but their pay-for-bed fellows mostly refuse to use them, keeping alive the deadly risk of AIDS and other sexually transmitted diseases.

"The women cater mainly to truck drivers and ferry operators spending nights at Daulatdia before crossing the river to Dhaka. Clients also include rail passengers, businessmen and students.

"They pay 150 taka ($3.09) for sex and 1,200 taka for a whole night. Charges vary depending on the girls' age and body shape.

"Most prostitutes conceive at the brothel. They prefer baby girls to boys. "The prostitutes are delighted when they give birth to female children because they can in turn feed them in their old age by picking up a sex job," Monira said.

"The Daulatdia prostitutes, required by law to be licensed, react angrily when NGOs describe them as sex workers. They prefer to be called sex slaves.

"But the Daulatdia women dream of escaping sex." Rezia Khatun was sold to the brothel by her husband, Nurul Islam, 35 years ago. She is now a Bariwali, meaning that she owns one shed with several rooms that she hires out to prostitutes.

"This is the lifetime dream of many brothel girls, like me," Rezia said. "This is one guarantee that you will not starve even if your daughters abandon you in old age," the 50-year-old said.

"I now have an income (outside sex). Fifteen young prostitutes pay me 30 taka per day each as rent." ($1=48.5 taka)

3/5/99

Last Day of Science Writers Workshop. Judging from feedback, it went well, but that is not to say that there is not considerable room for improvement.

The opposition is planning massive demonstrations late in the afternoon and my program is cut by a couple of hours because it is feared I might not be able to return to my guest house until very late in the evening without the risk of severe damage to my car and life and limb. Then, there is the distinct possibility of power outages which would leave me stranded at the office without air con for some time. And it is *krub gorum* (very hot).

Nayeem reports that he fell ill yesterday from something he ate. There is a team of Thomson people here for a seminar on child health issues that will be held on May 5-6 at the Sheraton. He has been in planning sessions all week with the Thomson team. Then, there is a small financial crisis. It seems BCDJC has gone over budget for the Child Health Seminar due to a miscalculation. Funds were allocated and dispersed on the basis of a one-day program and they have committed themselves to two. And you pay through the nose for the air con and the ambiance at the Sheraton.

4/5/99

Opposition leader Begum Khaleda Zia yesterday threatened to topple the government with a mass siege of Dhaka and called for a nation-wide strike and a cross-country march later this month.

Speaking at a rally before 8,000 supporters in Dhaka, the former prime minister called for a half-day strike on May 13 and a three-day march, beginning May 16, from the capital to Panchagarh, 280 miles to the north.

After the rally, organized by her Bangladesh Nationalist Party (BNP), Khaleda led thousands of supporters in a street march that turned violent at sunset when gunshots were fired and dozens of bombs exploded, triggering a stampede, according to witnesses . About 20 people were injured.

*　*　*

Meanwhile, the number of people being held by the police in its countrywide anti-terrorist drive now exceeds 13,000 with 210 illegal arms confiscated, according to *The Independent,* which leads with the story.

*　*　*

There is a story in a Bangla newspaper today that criticizes NGOs for solving too many of Bangladesh's problems from poolside at the Sheraton and Sonagaron, the top five-star oases in town. I will be attending a seminar tomorrow at the Sheraton on child health care issues partially sponsored by the Thomson Foundation. Bathing suits are optional

5/5/99

At least 30 people were injured in a battle between rival workers at a jute mill near Dhaka yesterday. Police said they used batons and tear-gas to disperse the groups fighting over trade union disputes at the Adamjee Jute Mills, 16 kilometers from Dhaka.

Among the injured, at least two were treated in hospital for bullet wounds.

The workers used home-made bombs, machetes and knives in the battle, which raged for hours. Three workers were killed and more than 100 injured in similar clashes at the mills on April 12.

✳   ✳   ✳

Power disruptions were so severe yesterday that stock exchange traders were up in arms in the pits. It was a hairy situation: More than the free-fall market could bear.

The heat was so intense it caused my head to shed five loads.

Attended opening day of Thomson-sponsored Workshop for Editors and Health Professionals at the Sheraton. Invited Rupa to lunch during the break so as not to miss my Bangla lesson.

✳   ✳   ✳

In retrospect, my Science Writers Workshop suffered from miscommunication. I was led to believe the participants had considerable science backgrounds because they had been working the science beat at their respective news organizations for from three to five years. Well, the latter was true, but, with the exception of one participant, none of them had a basic background in even high school science. They could not define the Greenhouse Effect, Acid Rain, Aquifers, the Ozone Layer, etc. So much of what was said I fear was over their heads. Nevertheless, to a man, and two women, they all came up to me and said how much they had learned during the week-long sessions.

6/5/99

The first serious rain since my arrival came to Dhaka overnight in the form of thunder-squalls. It has alleviated the heat somewhat.

I'm off to Saidpur/Sayedpur early tomorrow for a four-day Journalism Primer. Some 20 or more rural trainees from the local

Press Club will be on hand. The town is way up north near India and said to be within sight of the Himalayas.

* * *

A police Inspector General has caused something of a stir by suggesting that citizens be awarded 10,000 taka ($200) for bringing in a terrorist. A leading opposition party member jumped on the remark and said it was not clear whether the police wanted the terrorist dead or alive. If dead, it would turn the country into a killing field, he said. If alive, it still encouraged a citizen to take the law into his/her own hand. What a farce in a land with little in the way of law and order.

Royal Bengal Tiger

Hidden Agenda?

Mahfuz Ullah

7-12/5/99

My first surprise in Saidpur (some spell it Sayedpur) was the weather. It was cool in comparison to the furnace that is Dhaka. A light breeze greeted us (Mahfuz, Azfar, and myself) on arrival and the flat farmland, greened from recent rain, extended its hospitality to our eyes. A banana-colored press car whisked us to our government guest house where the rooms were large and provided with ceiling fans, air conditioner, and mosquito netting. A friendly spider or two, some large crickets, and a number of fast lizards shared the accommodations.

In the evening of the first day, after an opening workshop session, we visited a Biharis refugee camp. There are several in Saidpur and each camp houses several thousand refugees, who one day hope to be repatriated to Pakistan.

The Biharis, who migrated from India's Bihar state to East Pakistan, following the 1947 partition of British India, have remained stateless since Bangladesh became an independent nation in 1971. There are 400,000 Biharis living in such camps.

On a scale of one to ten with ten being the highest, the camp we visited rated 2.5 on the conditions scale. A 2 am fire about a month back had destroyed half the camp and new bamboo living huts were in the process of being built. Each living space was about 8" x 8" and meant to house a family of five. The smell of open sewage competed with charcoal kebabs.

The camp had no school or medical facilities. While we toured the camp, I noticed a funeral procession in progress. A woman had lost her husband to a liver disease. She carried a young baby in her arms behind the funeral wagon.

There were many children in the camp and they appeared adequately dressed and fed. I was told that second-hand clothing was cheap and abundant. These Urdu-speaking people live in the hope of one day returning to a better life in Pakistan, but there may not be any better life.

Mahfuz, co-trainer for our Journalism Primer, has suggested a way to curb the population explosion in Bangladesh—decree that all males must wear pants while banning too easily dropped sarongs on a moment's arousal. Given the male attention span, this just might work.

My second surprise in Saidpur was that the twenty participants (not a woman among them) who showed up for my Journalism Primer course turned out to be relatively wealthy part-time rural correspondents with, for the most part, ten to twenty or more years experience. I had been led to believe they would be novices or apprentices at the trade. When I asked the question, "What is news?," one participant rattled off seven text book answers without blinking an eye.

The notion has crawled into my head that workshops and possibly lectures could serve as a cover for another agenda. These training activities allow for relatively unrestricted travel around the country and are suspicion free gatherings because of international sponsorship and the immunity generally accorded journalists. It also has occurred to me that Bangladeshis have become experts at extracting money from foreigners and then using it for something other than what it was intended. Alas, perhaps I've read too much of Machiavelli.

At Mahfuz's insistence, we drove more than an hour ostensibly to see an artificial resort lake. We arrived just in time for a thunder squall that brought wind gusts to 35 knots or more per hour and heavy rains and bolts of lightening. On the drive back to the guest house, I was informed that a meeting had been arranged for me to visit a local Press Club in a nearby town where I was expected to talk for about an hour. The power, of course, was out when we arrived and the proceedings advanced in candle light.

Mahfuz is beginning to seriously irritate me. He is attempting to control me, the workshop, and what I do and see in my down time.

He is an avowed communist. He confided to me that he wants to overthrow the government here by a Maoist-style guerrilla revolution. He also is vociferously anti-American., partly because he was once denied a visa to visit the US.

Mahfuz, 52, has been described by Nayeem as being "the best trainer in Bangladesh," but I find him to be a long-winded pompous ass. He has very few positive, encouraging remarks for class participants and likes to leave the impression that he is the Superior Being from Dhaka. He heads the Bangladesh Centre for Sustainable

Development, which, among other things, is a clipping service. I gather his funding comes mainly from the European Union. Given his avowed political aims, I find his running such an organization rather ludicrous. I also find his stated political objectives at odds with my mission to support a free and independent press here.

Mahfuz, the Machiavellian Maoist Mouse that Roared, and I clashed verbally several times outside the confines of the workshop and our increasingly strained relationship has added an unneeded level of tension to the proceedings.

Mahfuz, who also was co-trainer for my recently concluded Science Writers Workshop, was all over me about the bombing of the Chinese embassy in Belgrade. He is convinced the Chinese government will eventually triumph in its ideological struggle with the US.

Meanwhile, Nayeem has informed Mahfuz that he will not be flying from Dhaka as planned to attend our closing ceremony. It seems he has a funding crisis with the Swedes who have informed him that monies promised for his program may have to be delayed because of the large concentration of emergency aid committed to Kosovo refugees.

Following our closing workshop ceremony, attended by some thirty local dignitaries, including the District Commissioner who handed out graduation certificates, our departure for Dhaka the following day was cancelled because of a countrywide 8-hour hartal. Mahfuz suggested we drive to the border with India and have a look see. It would only take an hour and fifteen minutes to the border, he assured me several times.

The trip took more than six hours, four and a half hours of which Mahfuz talked non-stop in Bangla. The head of the Saidpur Press Club came along for the ride.

When we arrived at the border, I was informed that Mahfuz and his Press Club colleague intended to interview the head Customs Inspector at the border point.

I sat outside in the car and waited, and waited. Smugglers, mostly women, came and went—drugs, textiles, and other contraband under their saris, babies in their arms, talking of mangoes and Michael Jordan to their pimps.

Finally, Mahfuz emerged with his entourage and we all took a walk in the twilight along the railroad tracks within easy gunshot of the Indian border guards. I fell on a wet stone and bruised my knee on the track. I ended up with a muddy white polo shirt and the embarrassment.

Then, Mahfuz and company retired for tea and I sat in the car with the driver and waited and waited.

Eventually, someone knocked on the window and passed through a sizable plastic bag of goods which was placed between my legs. I never did find out what was in the bag, but I suspect it was either illegal alcohol, drugs, arms, or all three.

As I sat in the car, a story was breaking in Dhaka that some 120 deaths have been recorded recently from alcohol poisoning—the result of home brewing and random marketing.

By the time we reached the guest house, it was near 10 pm. A trip that had been supposed to take three hours had ended up taking more than eight. I was pretty angry and passed up dinner.

The following day, shortly before departure, we were taken to the small office of a weekly newspaper in Saidpur, coincidentally published and edited by the head of the Saidpur Press Club. The usually four-page ïindependentî newspaper carries mostly political news. It has a circulation of about 2,000. I discovered that the two prizes I had awarded at the closing ceremonies on behalf of the Knight International Press Fellowship Program for the best written profiles in Bangla by coincidence had gone to the two top lieutenants of the president of the Press Club. Mahfuz, of course, served as the judge for awarding the prizes, which, he said, no one deserved. Azfar commented that "it was a very small community, where everyone helped each other."

At the airport, six or seven men I did not recognize came to see Mahfuz off. He disappeared with them for about 20 minutes outside the airport lounge. Was the Maoist mouse secretly at work nibbling away at the swiss cheese of democracy?

I gave the two lovely bouquets of flowers given me by the class participants on departure to the Biman stewardess as I boarded the plane for the return flight to Dhaka via Rajshahi. The gesture gained me a wide smile and an extra serving of orange juice.

13/5/99

I'm informed that Mahfuz, the Machiavellian Maoist Mouse that Roared, is a high-level activist within the opposition Bangladesh Nationalist Party (BNP). He stands to land an important post within the government should the opposition come to power anytime soon. Saidpur and the surrounding area is a BNP stronghold. Mahfuz, as I related earlier in this journal, once served as a PIO officer in a prior Bangladesh government when the present opposition was in power. He was based in Calcutta for awhile and professed to me that he ran a spy ring there largely composed of Indian journalists. The ring had provided important information on Indian government activities for

Bangladesh intelligence on several occasions, he said. Voila! The Hidden Agenda.

*   *   *

Went to Dhaka University to meet with the chairperson of the Journalism Department. I'm scheduled to give two lectures at the university on the 15th and 16th.

Gunfire and bomb blasts are a near daily occurrence on campus. This is a particularly hot time given the opposition's plans for agitations for the rest of the month and beyond. I was escorted to the office by Azfar and two other colleagues from BCDJC who obviously were intended as my bodyguards. Processions and political rallies were in evidence as we drove through the campus to the Department of Mass Communications and Journalism building.

Dhaka University, considered by many to be the best institution of higher education in Bangladesh, has about 65,000 registered students. There are about 400 in the Journalism Department. Competition is stiff for placement. There are about 30 applicants for each place in the Department.

*   *   *

In catch up news, the former chief of Bangladesh's now disbanded tribal guerrillas has taken over as chairman of a regional council in the Chittagong Hill Tracts, ending suspicions that he might go back into the jungles to revive his 22-year-old war.

Jyotirindra Budhipriyo Larma, also known as Shantu Larma, submitted his joining letter to Hill Tracts Affairs Minister Kalparanjan Chakma in Dhaka. The formal takeover by Larma apparently ended a long-running deadlock over the Hill Tracts administration.

Larma flew to the capital from Khagrachhari hill town, where he has been living since his Shanti Bahini (peace force) rebels laid down

119

their weapons in early 1998 after the government and rebels had signed a landmark peace treaty.

The treaty ended a quarter century of separatist insurgency in the Hill Tracts, which border India and Burma. The insurgency claimed more than 8,500 lives, according to official figures.

*   *   *

In another significant development, Bangladesh's Supreme Court today stayed a High Court ruling that strikes (hartals), the most powerful weapon in the opposition's arsenal, are unlawful. The Supreme Court postponed implementing the High Court ruling for two weeks. It said the stay order followed a petition filed by Abdul Mannan Bhuiyan, secretary-general of the main opposition Bangladesh Nationalist Party (BNP), challenging the High Court ruling. BNP leader Begum Khaleda Zia has indicated she will not accept the court order until Sheikh Hasina is forced back into opposition. Some political observers believe the court ruling will cause increased political violence rather than diminish it.

*   *   *

Bought a second-hand copy of Salman Rushdie's book Midnight's Children. This winner of the 1993 Booker Prize is still banned in Bangladesh.

14/5/99

It's raining, it's pouring, this old man has been snoring. Six inches in 12 hours. The air is fresh, the temperature relatively low. The winds squally. A perfect day to prepare for lectures. People are swimming in the streets. Joy in mudville. I have renamed Dhaka, Downpour.

120

15/5/99

Gave a lecture in a small classroom at Dhaka University to about 20
graduate students on Democracy and the Media followed by a question and answer session. I gather the turnout was small because the
Mass Communications and Journalism Department is in the midst of
final exams this week. The session ran about an hour and a half. I
observed that two blue-shirted policemen armed with wooden batons
were stationed outside the classroom door during my deliberations.

Following my lecture, I had tea with the chairperson of the department, Professor Sitara Parvin, daughter of the President of
Bangladesh, Justice Shahabuddin Ahmed. She solicited my views on
whether pornography aimed at children and various web sites promoting violence on the Internet should be censored. I came down on the
side of no censorship.

16/5/99

Another lecture today at Dhaka University. This time on the Internet,
or what the third-year students like to think of as Electronic
Imperialism. The turnout is a little better than for yesterday's sleep
inducer. About 30 or so. The interest is keen, but one young lady in
the front row fell asleep about half-way through. I like to think she
had been up late studying for exams or maybe, life. Four students in
the class had computers, but none had ever accessed the Internet.
Nevertheless, they were absolutely sure this "tool of imperialism"
would widen the gap between the rich and poor. "How can we ever

catch up when each day we are falling behind," one student asked. And that was one of the easier questions.

Over post-lecture tea, Professor Sitara, who has one daughter and who is married to another faculty member in the Department, asked me to explain the dual standard applied in American foreign policy to such countries as Saudia Arabia vis-a-vis other undemocratic states in the Middle East. Oozing charm from every pore, I oiled my way out the door and disappeared into the oppressive heat that has returned to noontime Dhaka.

17/5/99

Thousands of opposition activists began a three-day motorcade march yesterday from Dhaka to the four corners of the country to push for the government of Prime Minister Sheikh Hasina to resign. In scores of cars, jeeps and buses, they began their 500-kilometer journey from Dhaka to the Panchagarh district, which borders on the state of West Bengal in India.

The leader of the Bangladesh Nationalist Party (BNP), Begum Khaleda Zia, began the march Sunday with warnings. "This march is to highlight the government's incompetence and failures," the former prime minister told her supporters in a brief speech on Dhaka's Paltan Maiden Avenue. She warned of massive action, including a call for people to march to Dhaka from all over the country to force the government to resign. "We are now in the streets to launch agitation against the government to save the country from perils. We will launch more vigorous agitation in the coming days. By God's grace, we will succeed."

Khaleda also accused the government of failing to safeguard the country's frontier, saying its sovereignty was "at stake." She has been critical of Hasina's Awami League government for having warmer relations with India.

Meanwhile, authorities put up tight security for the march, particularly in and around the Bangabandhu Bridge across the Jamuna River in northwestern Bangladesh, about 100 kilometers from Dhaka. Thousands of police and paramilitary troops were deployed there to protect the gas pipeline that runs beneath the bridge as the BNP convoy passes over it. The government had banned the convoy from passing over the bridge, but a last minute deal was struck with the opposition, and the ban was lifted.

At the same time, Khaleda's alliance partners — the Jatiya Party of former President Hossain Mohammad Ershad, Jamaat-e-Islami and the Islami Oikya Jote — began marches in different directions from the capital.

*　*　*

In continuing violence on university campuses, gun-battles erupted at Chittagong University over the weekend, leaving one student dead and 25 wounded in clashes motivated by politics. The shooting started when Jubairul Islam, a member of the Islamic student group Chhatra Shibir, was shot dead by supporters of the pro-government Chhatra League.

The death triggered widespread shooting on campus, leaving at least 25 wounded, police reported. Shibir is the student wing of the opposition Jamaat-e-Islami party. Shibir activists later ransacked the university's administrative building and shut down nearby colleges, local journalists reported. The student Shibir wing also called for an eight-hour general strike in the port of Chittagong and neighboring areas today in protest against Islam's death. Such actions have made getting a BA degree in this country a matter of six or more years.

At Rajshahi University, the student wing of the BNP has called a three-day strike beginning tomorrow as political tension builds on that campus. While I was away in Saidpur, Rajshahi saw several days of political violence when armed gangs terrorized officials of the local Water Board causing many to flee their homes along with their families.

✳   ✳   ✳

While politics remains a sticky wicket in this country, the World Cup cricket matches in Britain have dominated the front pages of the national newspapers above the fold. Bangladesh makes its debut today. I have been bowled over by the amount of coverage.

✳   ✳   ✳

I had a brief, reasonably cordial meeting with Nayeem this morning. It was a sort of one-way discussion of future training efforts. While no mention of Mahfuz was made, it was clear his shadow hung over Nayeem's remarks. In future, Nayeem, acknowledging in an off-hand way that he had heard of some discord on my recent trip to Saidpur, suggested that I find a suitable co-trainer myself through the interview and recommendation process. He also felt that I should write directly to newspaper editors giving guidance about the type of participants desired.

From this point on, it will be my responsibility to prepare for each workshop, select guest speakers, and formulate course content and outlines. It was suggested the next workshop might be on an environmental topic, such as the Sundarbans, or shrimp farming. Fair enough. But, of course, it will take more time to prepare for such courses.

124

I seem to have already completed most of the assignments planned for me on arrival. I have another session planned with the fleet-footed Nayeem tomorrow.

I'm thinking of shorter, three-day courses and perhaps working more with an interpreter. Also, I might experiment by advertising for participants with a desire to learn the trade. I would rather train participants off the street than jaded journalists being recycled by the system.

*　*　*

Resumed my Bangla lessons after a lay off of several days.

18/5/99

Bangladesh opposition leader Begum Khaleda Zia headed for her northern hometown of Dinajpur yesterday, as part of the opposition cross-country marches and rallies to pressure the government to resign. Khaleda led a convoy of hundreds of vehicles and was cheered by thousands whom she urged to help topple the government, according to wire service and newspaper reports.

It was the second of three days of marches and rallies which opposition parties were staging to pressure the government to resign and call early general elections. "The prime objective of our road march is to help people realize the need for a change of government. And such a change cannot wait for long as we need to rid the country of an inefficient and inept government," Khaleda, leader of the Bangladesh Nationalist Party, told a rally in the northern town of Bogra. "If need be, we will call for a march to Dhaka from all corners of the country to force the government to quit," Khaleda told her followers.

The next general elections are not due until 2001. Hasina, who has just returned from a visit to the Netherlands, has repeatedly said there will be no early elections.

*　　*　　*

Another bangla lesson. I have learned that Bangla is the fifth most spoken language in the world, behind Chinese, Russian, English, and French.

*　　*　　*

Stopped in at The Asia Foundation to make an appointment to see the director. But she was not in. Learned that the foundation has trained some 600 Bangladeshi journalists since 1992.

Visited the Forum for Environmental Journalists. They have about seventy members and have just received a $1 million grant to be spread over five years from the United Nations Development Program (UNDP). The purpose of the grant is to heighten awareness of environmental issues.

We discussed the possibility of collaboration on a workshop devoted to the Sundarbans and the reaction seemed positive. I talked to two of the organization's chief consultants, one of whom knew of the Knight Foundation and had recently been in Washington. They said they would discuss the proposal with the organization's president and vice-president, both of whom were out of the office at the time. The deal basically would be that I would provide the training and the Forum would provide a field trip to the region and the participants from their pool of members.

Visited The High Commission of India Library to research books on the Sundarbans. No luck. There was one book on tigers, but it had very little useful information. It seems there are very few books avail-

126

able here on the Sundarbans and a check of Amazon.com disclosed all seven of their books on the topic were out of print.

Stopped at a couple of bookstores in an attempt to order a book on the Sundarbans printed in India, but came up empty. It takes three months or more for delivery.

Treated myself to drinks and a buffet dinner at the Pan Pacific Sonagaron Hotel.

19/5/99

The opposition's long march is over. Thousands of activists returned to the capital today and failed to heed Mao's admonishment that revolution is not a tea party. Many put up their feet, took tea, and watched a World Cup cricket match in a brief respite from politics. Opposition leader Khaleda Zia has called for the government to submit to immediate elections and has promised more agitation on May 24.

* * *

Meanwhile, the police have announced that more than 26,000 terrorists have been apprehended so far in their nationwide campaign to restore law and order. Three additional detention tent camps have been set up to handle the large number of alleged criminals, activists, and troublemakers. A relatively small number of arms have been confiscated.

* * *

I have now been in Bangladesh for three months. It hardly seems more than three years.

The staff at BCDJC today began its move to the new offices uptown. The new offices will be known as the School of Communications and officially open June 1. Azfar, who will be the Director, has moved out of his squalid digs and will live on the premises from today. Nayeem plans to keep the downtown offices open for other Centre activities as well.

20/5/99

Went to visit an old world Italian villa today complete with a beautifully neglected garden set among tall shade trees—the new uptown School of Communications under BCDJC. Quite a surprise!.

The numerous interior second-floor rooms that will serve as class space smelled of fresh white enamel paint and the newly mopped marble/tiled floors suggested a past Colonial elegance. It was light and airy. A large enclosed vined balcony ran the front length of the building. Fascist speeches might be given off it or it could serve as a classroom if some way can be found to deaden the street noise that pervades the serenity of this upscale antediluvian oasis.

Azfar, the once hard-core Communist revolutionary, the son of a bourgeois chemist, talked of hiring a gardener and perhaps of doing some himself. His apartment consists of a large room over the sizable four-car garage at the back of the premises. He said he would miss his many friends from the old neighborhood, a near slum area I suspect. But he looks forward to quiet times writing about his passion, music. His new neighbor is the Speaker of the Bangladeshi Parliament who lives in the spacious villa next door. Gatsby, old chap, would have felt a kinship for this place on a tender night; or the Finzi-Continis.

A roof garden is planned over the School of Communications for cultural events and between class lounging. I visualized Azfar singing stirring revolutionary folksongs among the large earthen flower pots, a thatched cabin or two, and round umbrella cafe tables with Cinzano ashtrays stuffed with the cigarette butts of environmental reporters. There is a large amount of space above the school available for such an endeavor.

The school hopes to be operational by July 1. Water, however, may be a problem. There are several Western-style bathrooms and a kitchen. An engineering company rents the ground-floor space.

Nayeem and staff are consumed at the moment with the move and all "the little illegal details" associated with such an upheaval.

Another Bangla lesson.

*   *   *

Met with the young photographer Moung Shwe, who has traveled from the Chittagong Hill Tracts to Dhaka to attend a conference on Sustainable Development. He brought me photographs taken by him on the night of my audience with "the King," his grandfather, tribal chief Moung Shwe Eru Chowdhury. He said the situation back home was such that, if Shantu Larma, once the head of the guerrilla army known as the Shanti Bahini and who has just recently become head of the Chittagong Hill Tracts Council, does not succeed in getting the government to fulfill its peace treaty pledges, he and other tribal members would return to the jungles to resume the insurgency.

21/5/99

;An Islamic cleric ordered a teenage girl buried to the waist in mud and flogged 101 times with a bamboo cane for having premarital sex and inducing an abortion, police reported yesterday. The girl subsequently died. The police learned of the incident nearly a week after the death, because the cleric had threatened the woman's family with reprisals if they went to the authorities.

Bedi Begum, 18, the daughter of a poor farmer, had induced an abortion with herbal medicines she received from her lover in Batsail, a remote village in northeastern Sylhet district. The whereabouts of the 25-year-old man was not known.

The cleric called Bedi's act un-Islamic and ordered her before an unauthorized court of village elders. Although Bangladesh is a predominantly Muslim country, Islamic clerics have no legal authority to conduct trials.

Bedi, still weak and bleeding from the abortion, was buried up to her waist in the mud floor of her thatched hut and caned by three villagers who took turns, according to the the area's police chief, Abdullah Baki.

The cleric prevented Bedi's family from taking the girl to a hospital and she died the next day. Those involved in the crime fled the village. A similar death occurred in Sylhet in 1993 when Islamic clerics ordered a woman to be flogged 101 times for having illicit sex with a man. The woman committed suicide, unable to endure the pain and humiliation. Eleven people were sentenced to life imprisonment for causing her death.

Women's rights advocates maintain that, in the last six years, such floggings have led to the deaths of at least 60 women.

Meanwhile, the total number of suspected terrorists apprehended in the nationwide crackdown to restore law and order now exceeds 29,000 individuals with some 400 weapons confiscated.

22/5/99

Approved an ad for a free basic journalism course to run in two newspapers (English and Bangla) next week

Rupa failed to show up for my Bangla lesson.

Had a lengthy talk with Nayeem, my first in some time. He is preoccupied with the move to the offices uptown and the possibility that funding from the Swedish Government, meant to cover operational expenses, will be delayed because of a Swedish diversion of funds to aid Kosovo refugees. He will know the outcome in about two weeks time. If there is a substantial delay, he will have to drastically curtail plans and operations for the new School of Communications.

In addition, he is somewhat irritated with the USIS for backing out of pledges for assistance with programs without giving any reasons.

We discussed the problems involved with getting suitable participants to attend workshops. He disclosed that he is seeking funding for a field trip to the Sundarbans that would be incorporated into a workshop. He did not mention the source and I did not pry. He said he would know in a few days. He seemed pleased that we had established contact again. He is growing a beard that his young wife insists must be shaved off. This has Freudian overtones best solved by Kama Sutran practices.

Worked on a course outline for a Sundarbans workshop.

The feeling that I've aged considerably on this assignment was confirmed tonight at dinner. The reality check came at the end of my
meal when the fat waiter at the Spaghetti Jazz up at Circle II in
Gulshan asked me how old I was. I said one hundred and four.
Deadpan, he shot back: "I can't believe it. You don't look a day over
ninety." Flattery will get you everywhere. I left him a sizable tip. I'm in
my '60s.

23/5/99

Azfar informed me that after lunch he will leave by bus for his home
in Comilla where his wife needs immediate medical attention for a
recently discovered large painful tumor in her breast. He will be away
for a week. I wished him well with the results. He has no medical
insurance. His departure will delay somewhat the move to the new
offices.

Another Bangla lesson.

✳   ✳   ✳

Bangladesh, meanwhile, has put its border security forces on alert
following the discovery of Indian soldiers digging "trenches" close to
the northern frontier, a foreign ministry official stated. "Bangladesh
has formally protested against the digging of trenches by Indian
Border Security Forces (BSF) on Thursday," the official, Abu
Abdullah, commented. The Indian side responded that it was digging
"water channels" for a tea plantation, not trenches.

"Fear among the people of the villages along the border is mount-
ing as the Indians are continuing to dig trenches and massing troops,"
Colonel Kazi Kauser of the Bangladesh Rifles (BDR), the country's
border security guards, stated at the border check point of
Panchagarh. Six Bangladeshis and three Indians were killed when border forces exchanged mortar and machine-gun fire in the western
District of Kustia on April 19.

24/5/99

The opposition has changed its tactics from hartal to procession. They
will take to the streets again today in an attempt to disrupt life in the
capital once again. The processions allow offices to remain open for
business, but make it so difficult to move about the city that not much
business gets conducted. Violence remains lurking in the heat of the
emotional sun. A power outage occurred at the exact moment the
opposition took to the street. Such outages had eased in recent days.

*   *   *

Rajshahi, meanwhile, continues to be a hotspot in the hinterlands.
The patients and doctors at the Medical College there have become
hostages to a gang of terrorists who are conducting a "reign of terror"
within and outside the institution. Several doctors have been injured
and many others threatened with death by the marauders who come
and go at will.

*   *   *

The Daily Star reports that every year some 20,000 Bangladeshi women
die giving birth and from post delivery complications, one of the high-

est rates in the world. Some 600,000 women face complications during delivery, 90 percent of which occur at home with untrained help.

*   *   *

Bangladesh, on the low road so far, take on Scotland today in the chirping World Cup cricket fields.

25/5/99

Bangladesh beat Scotland to gain its maiden win in World Cup play. The country went wild. The newspapers are flooded with front-page coverage.

*   *   *

Despite a nationwide roundup of "terrorists" that now exceeds 32,000 individuals, Bangladesh police appear to be losing the battle for law and order. Gunmen around the country have pulled the trigger and vanished before police have been able to lift their heavy British-rule vintage Lee Enfield .303s, aim and, hopefully, fire.

During the last three years, there have been at least 2,000 killings, with nearly 200 in the last three months, mostly in this country's "wild west." Half a dozen gangs preach communist revolution and thousands of people have been injured in frequent attacks.

At least five policemen are killed every year. A victim's family gets 100,000 taka ($2,061) by way of compensation. There is only one policeman for every 1,260 people, while in many developing countries, including Pakistan, the police/public ratio is one to 400. While the police have arrested more than 32,000 suspects in their month-long drive, they have seized fewer than 600 weapons, mostly small-calibre guns, knives, and axes.

The police face modern weapons, including sub-machine-guns and automatic rifles. A four-man police patrol carries just one British-made Enfield 303 between them. And their rifles often fail to fire, a high ranking police inspector disclosed. Buying new weapons has been put on the back burner, largely because of perceived political allegiances.

Opposition political parties brand the police as muscle men for the government, while the government often believes some police to be agents of the opposition. Meanwhile, the people generally believe the police to have secret links with criminals and terrorists.

On the Brink
of Nuclear War?

26/5/99

Kashmir took centre stage again yesterday as India launched air strikes against guerrillas dug into mountains on the Indian side of the Kashmir line.

The region comprises the Hindu-majority dominated plains of Jammu, the mainly Muslim Kashmir Valley, and the predominantly Buddhist Ladakh region.

When the subcontinent was partitioned in August 1947, the Hindu ruler of Muslim-majority Jammu and Kashmir agreed to join secular India rather than Islamic Pakistan.

That year in October, India and Pakistan fought their first war over Kashmir, which lasted till December1948 and ended with a UN-brokered cease-fire.

China occupied the 14,670 square mile Aksai Chin portion of Ladakh in 1959. India says China illegally occupies that area as well as 2,000 square miles of northern Kashmir that Pakistan ceded to Beijing under an agreement in 1963.

In 1965, Kashmir became the arena for the next Indo-Pakistani war, which also ended with a UN-mediated cease-fire.

The two also fought in Kashmir in December 1971, but that war was fought mainly over Bangladesh when it was East Pakistan. The current line of control demarcating the Indian and Pakistani portions was accepted by both sides in 1972.

Pakistan has called mountainous Kashmir a nuclear flash-point after New Delhi and Islamabad carried out nuclear tests last May.

Tensions between the two sides, always high, were also heightened last year by mortar and artillery duels along the UN-monitored military control line, which divides the region into two-thirds to be ruled by India and a third by Pakistan.

Both sides' forces have fought off and on at the world's highest battleground, the 20,000-foot high Siachen Glacier in northern Kashmir. Sporadic fighting has taken place there since 1984, when India occupied an area that Pakistan said was under its control.

Since early 1990, the idyllic valley of Kashmir under Indian control has been the hub of a separatist revolt by Muslim militants New Delhi says are trained and armed by Pakistan.

Although the militants are known to have training camps in Pakistan, Islamabad denies the charge. It says it gives only moral and political support to their campaign, which police and doctors in Indian Kashmir say have killed more than 25,000 people.

Last May's nuclear blasts brought Kashmir into sharper focus. Western moves to ease tensions forced India and Pakistan to resume peace talks, which had been deadlocked since September 1997 in a row over how to tackle Kashmir. In addition, Pakistani Prime Minister Nawaz Sharif, who would be deposed later this year in a military coup, and his Indian counterpart Atal Behari Vajpayee signed a Lahore Declaration in February, which pledges the two countries to work for better relations and to try to solve the Kashmir dispute.

New Delhi regards the whole of Kashmir as an integral part of India, but Islamabad wants the predominantly Muslim Kashmiris to decide in a UN-mandated plebiscite whether to join Islamic Pakistan or Hindu-majority India. Some militant groups seek independence for Kashmir, an idea rejected by both India and Pakistan.

*　*　*

I'm in charge! Went to the office yesterday to find Azfar in Comilla, Mukur headed for Rajshahi, and Nayeem and family apparently on a tea plantation in Syhlet. Seems everyone's abandoned ship for a few days down time. Had a Bangla lesson.

27/5/99

GRANDFATHER's WOLVES

There was grandfather. His little grandson
often came in the evenings to sit
at his knee and ask the many questions
that children ask. One day the
grandson came to his grandfather with a
look of anger on his face.

Grandfather said, "Come, sit, tell me
what has happened today."

The child sat and leaned his chin on his
Grandfather's knee. Looking up
into the soft, white-bearded face and
the kind blue eyes; the child's anger
turned to quiet tears.

The boy said, "I went to the town
today with my father, to trade the stamps he
has collected over the past several
months. I was happy to go, because
father said that since I had helped
him with mowing the lawn, I could get
something for me. Something that I wanted.

I was so excited to go to the trading
store, I have not been there before. I
looked at many things and finally
found a metal knife! It was small, but
good size for me, so father got it for me."

Here the boy laid his head against his
grandfather's knee and became silent.
The Grandfather, softly placed his hand
on the boy's raven hair and said,
"and then what happened?" Without
lifting his head, the boy said, "I went

outside to wait for father, and to admire
my new knife in the sunlight. Some town
boys came by and saw me, they got
all around me and starting saying bad
things.

They called me dirty and stupid and
said that I should not have such a fine
knife. The largest of these boys, pushed
me back and I fell over one of the
other boys. I dropped my knife and one
of them snatched it up and they all
ran away, laughing."

Here the boy's anger returned,
"I hate them, I hate them all!"

The Grandfather, with eyes that have
seen too much, lifted his grandson's
face so his eyes looked into the boy's.
Grandfather said, "Let me tell you a story.

I too, at times, have felt a great hate for
those that have taken so much,
with no sorrow for what they do.

But hate wears you down, and does not
hurt your enemy. It is like taking
poison and wishing your enemy would die.

I have struggled with these
feelings many times. It is as if there are
two wolves inside me, one is
white and one is black. The White Wolf is
good and does no harm. He lives
in harmony with all around him and does
not take offense when no offense was
intended. But will only fight when it is
right to do so, and in the right way.

But, the Black Wolf, is full of anger.
The littlest thing will set him into
a fit of temper. He fights everyone,
all the time, for no reason.
He cannot think because his anger
and hate are so great. It is helpless
anger, for his anger will change nothing.

Sometimes it is hard to live with these
two wolves inside me, for both of
them seek to dominate my spirit."

The boy, looked intently into his Grandfather's
eyes, and asked, "Which one
wins Grandfather?"

The Grandfather, smiled and said,

"The one I feed."

Discovered While Dancing with e-mail Wolves...

Rupa, my Bangla teacher, has the smallest feet I have ever seen, one of the things one observes while learning to count by rote to sixty. One of her feet might easily fit in the palm of my hand. Her feet are not the result of any kind of fetish. Strange, because otherwise she tends toward pulchritudinous voluptuousness. She wears elegant silk saris to class, some actually designed and batiked by her husband as a hobby to relax from his medical practice.

28/5/99

The army has reported destroying 144 acres of poppy cultivation in the Bandarban region which I visited earlier on my brief foray into the Chittagong Hill Tracts. While such army operations have been conducted in the past, this report indicates that poppy growing is still alive and well. Certain areas in the region are almost inaccessible as the jungle abuts Burma. Heroin producers and traffickers come and go almost at will.

* * *

Meanwhile, the total number of suspects arrested in the nationwide crackdown on ìterroristsî has risen to more than 35,500 individuals with a little more than 500 weapons confiscated.

Dhaka doodle do! What would the sunrise be without its cock? Dhaka is a city without. Without electricity a good part of the time, without adequate drinking water, without much hope for its poor. For the most part, it is a city of slums and shanties. Oh, there are a couple of five-star hotels where NGOs prescribe their country's remedies poolside, the fashionable restaurant or two, the wide tree-lined boulevards choked with rickshaws and air-polluting three-wheeled "baby taxis," the fashionable business high-rises, a multitude of banks, a park or two, but for the most part Dhaka is a disaster waiting for another disaster with unpliable roads, dingy shop stalls, and dark forbidding lanes.

The stench of poverty fills the nostrils. The legion of beggars, Azfar, once complained to me, make more than he does, on average about 800 taka per week ($14). The vast number of slum dwellers squat in their own waste on patches of government land easy prey for heroin and cocaine dealers and those others who would also arm themselves for criminal and political activity.

Tall sheet metal fences blot out the offensive slum views from the road and the passing more affluent eyes. Let's pretend it's a construction site, or some secret government project. But Dhaka is not a city without a prayer. Thousands are entoned every day in the mosques. Who is listening from without?

29/5/99

A day spent working on course outlines.

Another Bangla lesson.

Muggy monsoon weather.

Chili dog, potato salad, and beer at American Mission Club on eve of Memorial Day celebrated by expats here.

30/5/99

As Indian and Pakistan maneuvered diplomatically to avoid a possible nuclear confrontation, Muslim freedom fighters opposed to Indian rule in the disputed Himalayan region of Kashmir vowed today that they would hold their positions in the face of Indian attacks, according to a Reuters dispatch. The freedom fighters said they planned to advance further into the Kashmir valley territory occupied by India.

The militants, under attack from Indian aircraft for a fourth day in the mountain heights in the Kargil and Drass sectors of Kashmir, vowed. "We are here to stay. We will not only hold our positions but our target is to advance further into adjoining areas," Fazalur Rehman Khalil, the central amir (chief) of the Harakatul Mujahideen told Reuters in a telephone interview.

India, meanwhile, estimated that its troops had killed more than 400 freedom fighters.

Abdullah Muntazir, the information secretary of another guerrilla group the Lashkar-i-Tayyaba, said the next goal of the joint Kashmiri militant forces was to occupy the Drass-Kargil highway and if that was successful they would launch an attack on the town of Kargil. He said four militant factions - Harkat-ul-Mujahideen, Lashkar-i-Tayyaba, Tehrik-i-Jihad and Mujahideen Al-Badar - had formed a joint command for the Drass-Kargil operation.

Muntazir said the area's hilltops, stretching some 18 to 21 miles, were important because they overlooked the Drass-Kargil highway — the only land route connecting the northern Ladakh and Siachen areas with the rest of India. Pakistan and India have clashed intermittently in the Siachen glacier for the past several years.

India accuses Pakistan of sending militants into its side of Kashmir and supplying guerrillas there. Indian officials today said one of the dead freedom fighters had documents that proved "beyond doubt" that he was a Pakistani soldier.

Pakistan has denied that it provides logistical or military support to the guerrillas and has vowed to shoot down any Indian aircraft that strays over its territory.

Muntazir said about 1,000 guerrillas were holed up in the mountains. He said they were not very concerned about fighter aircraft, but were worried about helicopter gun-ships. The guerrillas are armed with SAM-7, shoulder-fired guided anti-air missiles.

The militants said on Friday that they shot down two Indian Mi-17 helicopters. India says one was downed by a Stinger missile. Pakistan says it shot down two Indian jets on Thursday after they violated its airspace. India said one was lost to ground fire and another to mechanical failure.

✻   ✻   ✻

Mukur confided that his trip to Rajshahi to visit with family did not go well. His aunt died as he was en route by bus, a seven-hour journey. He plans to return next week for the funeral.

Another Bangla lesson.

✻   ✻   ✻

In a significant business deal, Occidental oil interests in Bangladesh have been bought out by the US-based oil and gas exploration giant

148

Unocal, which already has significant operations in nearby Burma and Thailand. Unocal appears to be gambling that Bangladesh's already significant gas reserves can be dramatically increased and that the government position not to export existing reserves will change.

✳   ✳   ✳

Meanwhile, Prime Minister Sheikh Hasina, speaking before the National Press Club, said the country's press now enjoyed complete freedom. But she warned that some misguided journalists continued to write reports that were far from the truth. She urged that journalists adhere to professional standards. In my travels throughout the country, I have heard of rural newspapers being shut down recently by the government because of anti-government editorial content.

✳   ✳   ✳

Then, The World Food Program has reported that 20 percent of Western donor food aid is lost from system "leakage" before it reaches the country's estimated 30 million "ultra poor."

31/5/99

The Kashmir conflict continues to escalate with all signs headed toward a full-scale war between India and Pakistan. Most analysts though seem to think neither side will resort to a nuclear exchange because proximity dictates both populations would suffer unacceptable losses. I hope they're right, as I'm not so far away, but the hotheaded temperaments on both sides tip the rational scale toward unpredictability. India, in leaderless limbo until elections in September, is essentially under military rule at the moment.

Fierce close combat between Indian forces and the guerrillas continues, according to wire service reports, as does artillery duels and air strikes along the Kashmiri border between India and Pakistan.

While the Muslim freedom fighters in Indian territory opposed to Indian rule in Kashmir are relatively few in number, perhaps a thousand or so, thousands more are preparing to enter the fray in the rugged mountains of Pakistan. These Islamic militants are training at dozens of camps on Pakistani territory.

These fighters, according to an Associated Press dispatch, give little thought to international concerns about a large-scale war erupting between the long-time arch rivals India and Pakistan, both of which exploded nuclear devices in underground tests a year ago. For the young freedom fighters in training, the war already is raging.

Zaki-ur Rehman Lakhvi, chief of Lashkar-e-Tayyaba, one of the most militant fighting groups, said there is no shortage of recruits. The mother organization of his group, Markaz-ud-Dawa-wal-Irshad, runs 2,200 religious schools across Pakistan where its students learn Islam and prepare for "jihad," or holy war.

"We train 600 to 700 men every month in the summer, and we have to turn many more away because we just don't have the facilities," said Mohammed Azam, an instructor at the Lashkar-e-Tayyaba training camp.

Politicians in Pakistani-controlled parts of Kashmir have openly acknowledged the presence of the religious freedom fighters on their soil. A lawmaker in Pakistan's Kashmir Parliament, Mian Ghulam Rasool, said thousands were ready to cross into Indian-controlled Kashmir.

Discipline is reportedly tough at Lakhvi's camps. The men, mostly 17 to 25, espouse a philosophy similar to the strict ways of the Taliban religious militia that controls most of neighboring Afghanistan. They preach a restrictive and austere interpretation of Islam. Most forms of light entertainment, including music and television, are banned. The men, all in untrimmed beards, do not allow photographs. They wear the traditional baggy pants and long shirt; Western clothes are forbidden. Their training includes instruction on sabotage techniques, shooting skills, and hit-and-run raids, as well as hours spent studying the Muslim holy book, the Koran.

On the diplomatic front, the Indian Prime Minister Atal Bahari Vajpayee has rejected an offer by the UN Secretary General Kofi Annan to send an envoy to broker a peace deal.

1/6/99

Bangladesh upset world cricket power Pakistan yesterday and headlines usually reserved for declarations of war were displayed by the print media. The prime minister declared today a half-day national holiday even as the Pakistani foreign secretary declared his country would use "any weapon" in its arsenal for defense if necessary in its conflict with India over Kashmir.

* * *

Rupa cancelled my Bangla lesson because of the cricket victory, but taught me how to say "congratulations" over the phone so that I can properly face the people I come into contact with.

* * *

The ad I took in two local papers offering a free one-week Basic Journalism Course has had results. More than 20 people have called to date. I have interviewed two and the quality of the candidates is surprisingly high. And they all seem enthusiastic. The response has energized the office and raised morale considerably. In addition, we have sent out press releases for other courses and I have written two appeals to editors to supply participants for a Journalism Primer for Women With Emphasis on Cultural Issues, and a Workshop on Oil and Gas Development Issues.

＊　　＊　　＊

Close combat, meanwhile, raged on the 15,100-foot high Tololing Peak through the night in what Indian military commanders said was a crucial battle against the guerrillas in Kashmir. The guerrillas reportedly seized strategic mountain positions in the Indian-held part of Kashmir earlier this month. India has hammered the guerrillas for a week with air-strikes. More jets flew sorties today while artillery shelled the mountains.

The fighting appeared to be spreading. Indian shells slammed into a high school today in the Pakistani village of Nagdar, 70 miles from the guerrilla mountain enclaves, killing 10 students, according to official reports. Six people were killed on the Indian side Monday when a shell hit a government building.

Pakistan's army claimed it repulsed three separate attacks by Indian troops along the disputed border, inflicting heavy casualties. There was no independent confirmation of these reports and it has been obvious that a propaganda war is being waged as well.

Guerrillas also control nearly a dozen smaller hills near the Tololing Peak, but Indian commanders told reporters their troops would not directly assault them. Instead they will encircle the positions and try to starve out the militant Muslim freedom fighters.

2/6/99

Azfar told me his wife in Comilla was fine. The painful lump in her breast has disappeared. No biopsy was performed. A board of four doctors, he said, diagnosed a rheumatic condition. This story seems a bit fishy to me.

Meanwhile, the police arrested Afzal Khan, an Awami League leader in Comilla who is also chairman of the Bangladesh Cooperative Bank today on charges of corruption. His followers blocked the Dhaka-Chittagong highway with trucks and buses, tying up traffic for the entire day.

Got a sudden pain in my gut late in the day.

3/6/99

.Couldn't sleep much last night because of the off again on again pain in my stomach. Suspect an ulcer aggravated by chili. Can't remember if I've had my appendix out. Have decided to call in sick.

✻　✻　✻

Political violence has returned to the front page. Two Ward Commissioners were murdered in Chittagong, one hacked to death and the other shot in separate incidences. There had been fewer reports of such violence in the last couple of weeks. This report comes as the ruling Awami League, reportedly torn asunder by internal strife, plans for three days of golden jubilee celebrations, beginning June 23. Some 100 foreign heads of state have been invited, including

Bill Clinton. He better bring his horn if he comes because it will be one big jam.

*   *   *

Meanwhile, some 2,100 miles away, a Muslim militant group today claimed that more than 200 Afghan mujahideen (holy warriors) were in forward positions in northern Kashmir fighting Indian forces alongside local freedom fighters. The Mujahideen joined local forces in the Kargil-Batalik sectors, according to Abullah Muntazir, information secretary of the Islamist Lashkar-i-Tayyaba, who spoke to a Reuters correspondent by telephone. Muntazir claimed it was the first time such a large number of Afghan fighters had been sent to the Indian side of disputed Kashmir. The group, he asserted, hailed from Afghanistan's Nooristan province and was led by Commander Abu Shoaib Nooristani.

Muntazir said the Afghans were Lashkar's allies from the days of Soviet occupation of Afghanistan and have volunteered to help Kashmiri militants in their "struggle against India." The Afghans' expertise in conventional warfare is expected to bolster the militants, most of whom have been trained in hit-and-run guerrilla tactics. Muntazir said the Afghans were also experts in fighting with "improvised weapons."

The Afghan fighters speak Nooristani, much different from the Persian and Pushto widely used by freedom fighters in Kashmir. This language is not easy for Indian forces to understand, and thus will conceivably put them at a disadvantage when monitoring communications

Heavy snow put a damper on some of the mountain combat today, but artillery duels between India and Pakistan continued along the so-called line of control in the lower valley areas.

4/6/99

The fighting between India and Islamic freedom fighters, now in its 10th day, continues in Kashmir with reports that some 2,000 to 3,000 more militants are poised to enter the fray from the Pakistan side of the line of control. In Islamabad, the umbrella group representing the guerrillas, the United Jehad Council, claimed Indian fighter jets were dropping cluster and napalm bombs in their attacks. An Indian military spokesman denied the claims.

Pakistani army officials estimate India has deployed some 30,000 soldiers to dislodge the estimated 600 militants who infiltrated the snowy peaks last month. India says it has killed around 400 guerrillas so far. The numbers are suspect all around.

An Indian police official, meanwhile, has been quoted as having said that his country suffered a "complete failure" when it came to gathering intelligence about guerrilla and Pakistani intentions.

The prospects for a diplomatic settlement to the conflict between the two nuclear capable countries appears increasingly bleak at this time.

* * *

Went to the office today, but no one was home at 10 am. Out praying no doubt. It is the Muslim equivalent of Sunday here. The weather is fine and the Bangladesh cricket team is due home from England to a heroes welcome. In a land that seldom has a reason to pause for joy, I am happy for the populous' moment in the sun. Flowers, smiles, and congratulations all around. Terrorism can wait till tomorrow.

155

5/6/99

Five thousands cans of beer on the wall. What should happen if all should fall? That's what happened yesterday when police. foaming at the mouth, jugged a lug for possession of the illegal froth in this Muslim country where alcohol is banned. Party time at police headquarters as another terrorist crumpled in the can.

*　　*　　*

India, meanwhile, has informed Pakistan that a visit by its foreign minister on June 7 to discuss the Kashmir issue is "inconvenient" at this time. Don't call us, we'll call you.

Leaving the relative security of their grim outposts in the high Himalayas, Indian forces face advancing over very hostile terrain. The freedom fighters are entrenched above vertical rock faces and along razor-edge ridges, where temperatures can plunge to minus 4 in the summer. The militants occupy strategic peaks on the Indian side of the cease-fire line with Pakistan. The peaks dominate a snowy mountainous region up to the perennially frozen Siachen Glacier, where Kashmir meets the Chinese border.

If India can expel the Muslim freedom fighters, it will likely have to reorganize its defenses to ensure the ridges cannot be occupied again, according to V.K. Raghavan, a retired Indian army general who has commanded troops in the area. That could mean building permanent outposts manned through the winter when temperatures can drop to minus 76 and when the peaks sometimes are buried under 20 feet of snow. The avalanche-prone Siachen Glacier reaches to 20,000 feet. Blizzards are sometimes accompanied by 200 mile-per-hour winds. While death or being wounded in combat is a daily occurrence, more troops fall victim to hypothermia, frostbite and a host of high altitude physical and mental ailments.

In winter, the weather gets so bad that helicopters can no longer fly and the outposts are cut off for months. Their only communication with military headquarters is by battery-powered radio sets. Batteries and men die.

The battle for the town of Kargil and the surrounding sector, meanwhile, could prove as costly as that for the Siachen peaks. Like Siachen, the Kargil mountain range has no roads. Helicopters must ferry food, mail, and medicine to the forward outposts.

The Pakistani army on the other side of the line of control faces no such problem, since they do not control the heights in the region and their posts are farther back in less hostile areas.

6/6/99

Three people have been let go at the BCDJC, two of them part timers. A sign of belt tightening? Perhaps. Expected Swedish funding has been delayed—for how long no one seems to know.   Mukur has returned from Rajshahi. His visit to attend his aunt's funeral coincided with a visit by the prime minister to attend an Awami League Golden Jubilee planning session and celebration. I have the feeling that I'm not always playing this game with a full deck. There is very little information offered about what is going on in respect to BCDJC beyond my own specific programs. Nayeem mentioned that he had a nibble from the Soros Foundation and plans to seek a loan. Would I support his application? Yes. He still plans to travel to the US in July to attend a Kettering Foundation-sponsored conference on promoting democracy at the grass-roots level. At my suggestion, he's working on a barter deal with Biman Airlines for a ticket to New York.

Another Bangla lesson.

7/6/99

A day of preparing for upcoming workshop entitled Women's Journalism Primer With Cultural Focus.

✻   ✻   ✻

Today, the FBI put Osama bin Laden on its "Ten Most Wanted" list. The U.S. has accused bin Laden of masterminding the deadly Aug. 7, 1988, bombings of our embassies in Kenya and Tanzania, which killed more than 200 people and injured thousands. Bin Laden is believed to be on the move again after falling out with his former hosts, the Taliban religious militia that rules Afghanistan. Washington says he is still in hiding in that country. Others have suggested he is on his way elsewhere — Somalia, Chechnya, even Iraq — preferably somewhere gripped by anarchy and rife with anti-US sentiment. In my upcoming novel, a work in progress, I have him hiding out in the forbidding, nearly impenetrable Sundarbans.

8/6/99

The Daily Star today reported on Page One above the fold that 210 "outlaws," responding to a government offer of amnesty, surrendered yesterday along with their arms at Jessore, the Tombstone of Bangladesh. *The Independent*, meanwhile, played the same story on the back page, but put the number of "extremists" giving up at 230. In what smelled to me like a government stage-managed event, one of the leading "outlaws" told the large gathering on hand at the Town Hall Maiden:"We have now realized that we were reduced to terrorists for achieving personal and heinous objectives in the name of Marxist and Leninist politics. But in reality, they (other, still at large, banned communist party leaders) have no relationship with Marxism and Leninism. We have been used to protect their personal gains and heinous designs." I almost wept at the thought of a used communist terrorist. I suppose the recently appointed Home Minister Mohammed Nasim did, too. He was on hand for the surrender ceremony.

The old cynic in me asked Nayeem what was really going down. "It's a legal ploy," he said. "It's been used by every government in power since Independence. Those that surrender in most cases have probably committed terrorist acts, even murder, for individuals or officials in power. The amnesty thus is a way of clearing any legal charges that may be pending against these terrorists, thus freeing them to commit more breaches of the law. Rehabilitation and return into mainstream society is in most cases unlikely."

"It's a political game," Mukur commented. "I myself once surrendered and turned in my .38 caliber pistol."

This discussion led me to ask if their was a substantial difference between what Bangla newspapers print and the material in the English-language press. Nayeem's answer was "yes." The English-language press, he said, caters to an elite, generally highly educated audience which serves in most cases the interests of the foreign community. In general, the reporting is of a higher caliber in terms of accuracy, but still many errors creep in. The politics are more subtle, more sophisticated, and biases are thinly disguised. The reporters, of course, are more highly paid. In the Bangla press, the stories are more "biting," more interesting generally, but the facts, even simple ones, are always suspect. For example, the Prime Minister recently was presented a bouquet by a student group while leading a procession in the streets. Twelve Bangla newspapers had the presentation occurring at different locations in the city,.

Some Bangla newspapers pay their reporters a living wage, but most do not. Survival thus depends on becoming a PR man for some interest or another. Often this revenue source is shared with the newspaper. Only bureau chiefs are generally paid outside Dhaka and there are not too many of those. As a general rule, correspondents in the field are not paid, thus stories from the countryside serve the interests of those who pay the reporters for coverage of an event.

* * *

Azfar informed me that there were now 42 responses to the ad for participants in our planned July Basic Journalism Course. The qualifications of those submitting applications for the 20 openings is extremely high. Many have advanced degrees, though not in journalism, and a fair number have worked in the past as reporters or editors.

* * *

In the continuing Kashmir conflict, India offered today to hold high-level peace talks with Pakistan this coming Saturday. There was no immediate word on whether Pakistan would accept.

9/6/99

The number of suspects arrested in connection with the nationwide crackdown on communist "terrorists and outlaws" has risen to some 47,000, according to the police. A Maoist rebel leader, Uday Shankar, and 12 other guerrillas where the latest to surrender under a general amnesty. The rebels, members of the outlawed Revolutionary Communist Party, gave themselves up in Khulna, 85 miles south of Dhaka. Meanwhile, one outlawed communist party, the Bangladesher Biblobi, issued a statement saying none of its comrades had surrendered and accused the government of "state terrorism" tactics.

Azfar says the total number of communist party members in Bangladesh is somewhere between 4 and 6 million, of these about a third are affiliated with outlawed parties. He says the non-banned Bangladesh Communist Party has no ideological bent at the moment and many of the members serve the corrupt and violent interests of influential individuals.

✳   ✳   ✳

Meanwhile, hundreds of Islamist Fundamentalists rallied in Dhaka today to oppose a planned visit to Bangladesh by Indian Prime Minister Atal Behari Vajpayee on June 19. "We cannot accept him because he led Hindu fanatics in the destruction of historic Babri Mosque in Ayodhya in 1992," Moulana Shaikul Hadis Azizul Hoque, president of the Bangladesh Khelafat Movement, told the rally. Hindu zealots demolished the 16th century mosque in northern Uttar Pradesh state and Vajpayee's Bharatiya Janata Party won power on a campaign to build a temple on the site. "It is also he who has launched a war against Mujahids and resorted to massacres in Kashmir," the Fundamentalist leader was reported as having said, amid chants of "Allahu Akbar" (Allah is great).

Vajpayee and Prime Minister Sheikh Hasina are scheduled to welcome passengers arriving from India on the first regular bus service between the two countries. The service between Dhaka and Calcutta, capital of India's eastern state of West Bengal.

"June 19 will be a black day. We will launch a tough movement on that day if Sheikh Hasina allows him (Vajpayee) to land on this soil," Hoque said. He warned the Bangladesh government "not to play with fire by hosting a man who has always insulted Muslims."

10/6/99

Nayeem is seeking to raise a million dollars for a newspaper launch. I have agreed to help him with a Business Plan.

*   *   *

Inflation here is running at 8.8 percent.

*   *   *

The opposition has called a countrywide dawn-to-dusk hartal for June 13 to protest the "anti-people" measures in the national budget, unveiled today.

∗   ∗   ∗

More than 3,000 "outlaws and terrorists" are reported to be still at large in the southwest.

∗   ∗   ∗

Is cricket like watching paint dry or peel?.

∗   ∗   ∗

The number of responses to my ad for participants in a basic journalism course this July has risen to 86.

∗   ∗   ∗

FBI Public Enemy No. 1 Osama bin Laden surfaced on Dubai television today and renewed his call for a Holy War against his Public Enemy No. 1, the United States. The 90-minute program was aired by a Qatar-based satellite channel and seen by millions of viewers in the Middle East, North Africa, and Europe. The al-Jazeera channel is the Arab world's most popular station. The place and time of the interview was unclear. A station source said the interview was several months old.

163

The Mastani Culture

11/6/99

$\int$ was introduced to a new term today: "Mastan." The old Bengali dictionary meaning of mastan was "one who is in the state of intoxication." But the contemporary definition of mastan is "an armed individual who uses force or terror to obtain something. The possession of arms is his source of strength."

The Daily Star yesterday devoted two full pages to an exploration of the Mastani culture, which has become a social disease of epidemic proportions in this country.

A decade or two back, mastans were associated with street urchins, but today they represent a powerfully destructive force abroad in the land and they are replicating themselves at all levels of society.

Some turn to the Mastani way of life because of a lack of education, others because of a lack of job opportunities, still others because of family engagement in anti-social activities, and many others because it is simply perceived as the easiest way to become rich in the shortest possible time. Mastans can be found at all levels of society. And they frequently can be found on university campuses.

A case in point is Chittagong, where 60 top terrorists are reported to be under the protection of 12 "god-fathers" of whom some are politicians from both the ruling and opposition parties. The fallout from this situation is the emergence of a political culture that is increasingly incorporating mastan power into mainstream politics. Election-rigging, hartals, political vengeance, etc., whether carried out by the ruling or opposition party, have a common denominator: dependence on mastans. Such interdependence not only breeds more violence, it legitimizes violence. The Chittagong model is common throughout the country, particularly in Dhaka.

Mastans are used, they do not rule or govern. This phenomenon lurks in the undercurrents of my impending Civil War hypothesis. The thrust of *The Daily Star's* well-researched contention, developed by the Centre for Alternatives, was that Bangladeshis are living in a Mastanocracy with little choice, not a Democracy.

12/6/99

An Indian military analyst has stated that while both India and Pakistan have delivery systems to launch nuclear weapons, neither side actually has developed a weapon sufficiently to the point where it is ready to launch.

According to Oxford Analytica, an international consulting firm, the United States' behind- the-scenes efforts to limit the Kashmir confrontation is directed toward getting the signatures of India and Pakistan on the Comprehensive Nuclear Test-Ban Treaty by September. India, in this view, could gain important support for some of its wider international goals (such as a UN Security Council seat) if it adopts what the international community views as an intelligent position towards the conflict. Moreover, India's own strategy in Kashmir depends on the issue not becoming "internationalized" — which requires the goodwill of the United States and would almost inevitably happen if the present conflict becomes a war.

Pakistan's strategic ambitions are diametrically opposed. It is seeking to "internationalize" the issue through UN intervention— and may have been encouraged to intensify the pressure on India by recent events in Kosovo. Pakistan is heavily dependent economically on the United States and only recently avoided bankruptcy. Washington thus far has shown no signs of reneging on its long-held opposition to assuming a mediation role in Kashmir — which would mean forcing India to the negotiating table. Pakistan is unlikely to have the means to change this. Moreover, Islamabad's other principal foreign allies — China and Saudi Arabia — also have their own reasons for wishing to see the conflict contained. With Tibet in mind, Beijing would not want Kashmir to appear on any international agenda. Similarly, Saudi Arabia is aware that a war with India would jeopardize the domestic security of India's 120 million Muslim citizens.

Ultimately, both sides have much more to lose than to gain from permitting the conflict to escalate towards full-scale war. However, interest groups within each country appear to have ambitions of their

own which could sustain confrontation. Military miscalculations on
the ground could cause events to move in undesirable directions.

13/6/99

Hartal day, the first for some time.

Time spent writing and preparing for Women's Journalism Primer
With Cultural Focus. We now have at least 10 participants.

14/6/99

Hartal toll: One dead and at least 200 injured, several from bomb
blasts in downtown Dhaka and Chittagong. This was interpreted by
the press to mean a "relatively peaceful" strike. Processions and rallies
have been banned at Chittagong University until June 30 in an effort
to stem the political violence there. The opposition has called a
"protest day" for June 18.

✻ ✻ ✻

The peace talks between India and Pakistan have ended in stale-
mate. The fighting over Kashmir continues.

✻ ✻ ✻

It seems my letter to editors of various newspapers requesting participants for the Oil and Gas Development Issues Workshop has caused
offense to cultural sensibilities. A few have refused to send participants
because I asked to "interview" the selectees. They interpreted that as

testing them. I had to call each editor and straighten out the misunderstanding.

15/6/99

Now here is a man who's never been burned. A local matchmaker maintains he has not been able to strike the flame of love for himself. "I have spent my life finding matches for young men and women," Manu Miah told the *Janakantha* newspaper. "I started my career at the age of 18... I am now 87 and still a bachelor. Rather I found solace in solace in finding burning matches for others," he said. Manu has arranged the weddings of more than 16,000 couples. Wooden matches, of course.

16/6/99

Downtown Dhaka thieves have a new twist. Roving gangs of some 30 or more youths are robbing rickshaw riders at knife-point in broad daylight when they get caught in a traffic jam. The gangs fan out when they spot a jam; three muggers to a rickshaw. The police as yet have done nothing to stop the mass robberies which are becoming more frequent.

* * *

A two-day strike by workers at some 300 jute mills ended yesterday. The workers, pushing for higher wages, withdrew barricades on a highway and train lines between Dhaka and Chittagong that paralyzed transportation. Private mill-worker unions called the 48-hour blockade and strike to protest against a delay in pay rises recommended by a 1991 wage commission. The commission had recommended minimum wages for industrial workers be raised to 1,000 taka ($20) a month, but they are still being paid less than 900 taka. The unions threatened more disruptions if their demands were not met.

17-19/6/99

The three-day Journalism Workshop for Women With Emphasis on Cultural Events went reasonably well. Sixteen participants were in attendance, though only 14 received course certificates. I think it could be called a success judging from the evaluation forms. I was a one-man show. We discussed art, poetry, drama, dance, music, and literature in general in addition to the fundamentals of journalism. I have invented a new art form which I've dubbed "segueism."

The women participants, all full-time practicing journalists, were a pleasure to serve—alert, bright, bubbly, asking relevant questions. They leave the men well behind by comparison.

At the conclusion of the course, they gave me a big bouquet of flowers and a framed tapestry depiction of local life. So on to my next five-day Workshop on Oil and Gas Development Issues, beginning on June 26th.

20/6/99

Indian Prime Minister Atal Behari Vajpayee visited Bangladesh yesterday to inaugurate the first bus run between the two countries. He was given a red-carpet welcome on arrival as police held back hundreds of Islamic protesters asking him to go back.

The Indian Prime minister, accompanied by Foreign Minister Jaswant Singh and senior officials, was met at Dhaka airport by Prime Minister Sheikh Hasina.

Authorities deployed some 3,000 extra police and paramilitary troops to ensure tight security . Hard-line Muslim religious groups here refer to the Indian leader as a Hindu fundamentalist with strong anti-Muslim feelings.

Just before sunset, Vajpayee and Hasina jointly received two bus-loads of passengers who had traveled to Dhaka from Calcutta. Just a few blocks away, an estimated 8,000 activists of the fundamentalist Jamaat-e-Islami party held a noisy rally. Police laid a tight cordon around the rally so the Islamists could not try to run towards the buses, according to eye-witnesses.

Bangladesh has said it is willing to mediate over Kashmir, but India wants the conflict to be resolved bilaterally.

Meanwhile, political violence keeps apace with an Awami League leader chopped to death yesterday in Jessore, while the day before another AL leader was killed by strangulation in Kishoreganj. And there were two young political activists shot to death today in downtown Dhaka.

＊　　＊　　＊

Another Bangla lesson. In my dreams, my teacher and I dance the Mango Tango before a demanding audience of 39 consonants and 11 vowels. When the moment is ripe, we do the Bangla dip. It's quite a dance.

21/6/99

Some pieces to the Nayeemul Islam Khan mosaic, or assorted tintinnabulations. Nayeem attended Dhaka University where he earned an MA in Mass Communications and Journalism in 1983. After Nayeem, described as a "radical" in his younger student days, became editor of the daily *Ajker Kagoj*, a newspaper whose vision was his, he had a financial falling out with the Publisher, a former army lieutenant colonel who bankrolled the paper's launch in 1991. It seems over time, Nayeem, flush with an enlarged ego over the paper's editorial success, became too independent. He often did not consult with the Publisher, described as a pretty reasonable man, over editorial changes and financial matters, irregularities really. Nayeem is "creative" when it comes to finances. He was on a power trip. This situation came to a head when Nayeem demanded a 50 percent share of the enterprise for himself and the employees. The Publisher offered a third stake, but Nayeem refused. About 200 of the Publisher's goons came by the paper's office one night and physically routed Nayeem and his followers.

Nayeem moved on in 1992 to become founder and editor of the daily *Bhorer Kagoj*, which also enjoyed a good reputation, but Nayeem chafed at his lack of control and was branded a "maverick" by many of

174

those influential in the publishing world. His time as king of the press hill ended in April of 1993 when he either quit or was forced out. His ability to find work at the top editor level diminished.

One of Nayeem's early political heroes was Sheikh Mujibur Rahman, who was assassinated in 1975 shortly after Independence (1972) and whose daughter Sheikh Hasina is now Prime Minister and head of the Awami League. At some point it seems, Nayeem's political preference switched to the opposition Bangladesh Nationalist Party (BNP), led by Khaleda Zia. But the impression I get is that, while very savvy about political undercurrents, Nayeem is not committed to one party or the other and is comfortable in both the government and opposition camps. He serves the tiger of entrepreneurship at the moment. He is a bit of a peacock, four silver rings on his hands, and quick to take offense if challenged in any way.

He owns two cars, a plot of land on an island in the Bay of Bengal, collects knick knacks, is fond of inspirational sayings which adorn wooden plaques in his office and home, and is looking to buy a condo or the right piece of real estate in Dhaka. His wife of the moment, his third, is in her early twenties and a student at Chittagong University. Nayeem is interested in women and their causes and I often see him carrying scholarly books about their psychological and sexual natures.

Nayeem's first marriage to Taslima Nasrin, the militant feminist writer now in exile in Sweden, lasted about two and a half years. She was depicted as very attractive but a little psychotic. She apparently was sexually abused as a child. According to Amnesty International, she returned to Bangladesh last September after four years in exile. Calls for her arrest by Islamic Fundamentalists were ignored by the police, but she felt unsafe and went back into exile. She has a reputation for sexual promiscuity and also a foul tongue and pen.

This week Nayeem, who just turned 40, confided to me that he missed the daily rough and tumble of the newsroom and would like to return as editor one day to the fray. Hence his drive to raise a million dollars to start a new newspaper.

Today, he is said to be locked in a three-way battle with the Thomson Foundation people and another NGO for control of a project aimed at helping children at the grassroots level. Nayeem feels the project is his and that the two other principals are attempting to relegate BCDJC to a backseat on the project bus. He is livid over this.

Another Bangla lesson. My proficiency is improving. We do the Mango Tango. Life is one big dip. Forgive me Argentina.

22/6/99

The monsoon season has begun in earnest. Torrential rain in southeastern Bangladesh has already caused severe flooding in the port city of Chittagong and the resort town of Cox's Bazar inundating some 60,000 homes and killing two with three persons missing. The water is knee deep and rising in the low-lying areas. The entire country, including Dhaka, has been experiencing heavy rain. Gusty winds blowing at up to 30 miles per hour have accompanied the rains in the southeast.

*   *   *

The opposition has called another dawn-to-dusk hartal for July 8 to protest for a second time the national budget which they deem "anti-people" and engineered to serve the rich and corrupt.

23/6/99

The daily *Janakantha*, a large circulation Bangla newspaper, has carried an exclusive report citing Indian and Bangladesh intelligence sources that says Pakistan's Inter Service Intelligence agency has been supporting a group of terrorists in West Bengal that have plans to infiltrate the northern region of Bangladesh with the mission of creating anarchy there. The Indian police have arrested about 50 of the some 1,000 terrorists who are led by a "notorious" criminal, Abdul Karim Tunda. Mukur smiled at mention of the criminal's name. "I used to be his boss," he remarked. Text of the article follows:

ISI & Tunda Plan to Create Anarchy

Inter Service Intelligence (ISI) of Pakistan is using Abdul Karim Tunda, a notorious terrorist, as a pawn in mobilizing Bangladeshi terrorists to create chaos in the country.

Risaldar (Sergeant) Mosleh Uddin, tried in absentia, convicted, and sentenced to death in the murder case of Sheikh Mujibur Rahman (in 1975), is acting as the chief associate of this chessman. Tunda is now busy organizing Bangladeshi terrorists.

Tunda has already established contact with approximately one thousand terrorists who are presently hiding in Calcutta and its suburbs. He is planning to send them back to Bangladesh, provided with firearms, to disrupt the existing equilibrium. He is operating on behalf of ISI of Pakistan. Their main objective is to overthrow the elected government of Bangladesh.

Tunda has been engaged in this activity for quite sometime. With this end in view, he is keeping liaison with Risaldar Mosleh Uddin, presently hiding in India. A few weeks back, he also met a couple of Bangladeshi businessmen. Their meetings took place in a well-known hotel and in a fundamentalist hideout at Khidirpur. There they discussed mainly how those arms were going to be smuggled into and used in Bangladesh.

Intelligence agencies came to know about these talks and attempts were made to to arrest them. But they failed.

In the meantime, Tunda, in association with some Bangladeshi terrorists, has already committed some crimes in Calcutta and the neighboring areas.

Indian police became aware of this activity from statements given by arrested Bangladeshi terrorists. West Bengal police have formed a special unit to arrest Tunda on sight, and other Bangladeshi
terrorists as well, under authority of the central government of India.

Sujoy Chakrabartee, an adjunct commissioner of Calcutta metropolitan police, is the chief of the unit. Orders have gone out to all district police Supers in West Bengal to maintain keen surveillance
in border areas. Bangladeshi intelligence agencies are giving full support to this newly formed unit.

According to reports from various sources, more than a thousand die-hard terrorists have fled across the border due to the recent Bangladeshi police combing operations. Most of these terrorists in hiding are from Kustia, Chuadanga, Meherpur, Jessore, Khulna and Rajshahi. As they are professional terrorists, it was easy for Tunda to contact them. At least 50 of these terrorists have already been arrested in different locations in West Bengal. Source: The daily *Janakantha*, 16 June 1999.

24/6/99

The government of Bangladesh, one political wag commented, "is like a blind man searching for a black cat in a dark room."

*   *   *

Meanwhile, Western defense analysts, including those from the International Institute of Strategic Studies, and diplomats reportedly believe India may be forced to widen the Kashmir conflict in the days ahead to rid the Himalayan peaks of so-called freedom fighters. The shape of India's response to what it calls an invasion by Pakistan-backed infiltrators should become clear in coming weeks if India is to rout the enemy before snowfall in August makes terrain impassable.

Defense specialists believe India has two choices — to cross the Line of Control to attack the infiltrators from the rear, cutting off their supply lines, or to open another front along its international border to force Pakistan to pull the infiltrators back. In the last of the two countries' two wars over Kashmir, in 1965, India opened a second front against Pakistan along the Punjab border as pressure mounted in Kashmir.

Some analysts believe that New Delhi would favor the first option — a limited assault across the cease-fire line, far from the cameras of the international media.

Diplomats believe that either option could bring full-scale war because Pakistan would instantly seek world condemnation for an attack across its borders.

Analysts believe that India has to clear the insurgents from current positions because they command the strategic Srinigar-Leh highway which India uses to supply troops in Kashmir and on the Siachen glacier battlefield to the north. Current positions give the insurgents the capability to interdict the highway. They are said to be well armed with mortars, machine-guns, and missiles. They also are in a position to guide Pakistani artillery fire through observation.

25/6/99

Day spent going over notes for my five-day Advanced Reporters Workshop on Oil and Gas Development Issues, which opens tomorrow. Twelve to 14 participants expected.

John Kincannon, director of the USIS operations here, is guest speaker on the second day. There will be five speakers overall, the other four representing the geological framework, the arguments for conservation or non-export, the Indian factor, and the economic fallout.

26-30/6/99

"Should Bangladesh put up a new sign at the airport to promote tourism in the new millennium," one of the guest speakers in my Advanced Reporters Workshop on Gas Development Issues cynically asked? "It might read,

'Welcome to the 19th Century.'"

His point was that to not export gas the country would be like an ostrich putting its head in the sand. The caustic remark came during a heated debate that is presently consuming the business and political elite in this foreign currency starved nation: To export gas, or not That was the question before the 12 participants, all mid-level reporters on daily newspapers in Dhaka covering the energy sector. Whether tis nobler of the mind to suffer the slings and arrows of outrageous fortune and poverty by keeping an "unknown" quantity of reserves for domestic use, or, by allowing International Oil Companies (IOCs) to drill exploratory wells, take arms against a sea of troubles and end them. That was and is the question.

The word "export" here is really a euphemism for "to India."

There was much conundrum discussion during the five-day deliberations about which came first, the chicken or the egg, the latter representing the size of the gas reserves, which ranged from dinosaur to quail depending on how flatulent the estimate. The United States and International Oil Companies represented the foxes trying to get into the hen house. One has to have faith that the Ham(let) omelet came first.

It is my opinion, based on participant feedback, that this workshop was my most successful to date. At least four articles by participants based on the remarks of the five guest speakers were printed by their respective newspapers. All came away saying they were better informed on the sensitive political and scientific issues involved.

John Kincannon, director of the USIS and Deputy Chief of the US Mission here, spoke on the second day.

The workshop had its humorous moments. On the last day, during an informal discussion session between scheduled talks, one participant asked me whether CIA agents ever posed as journalists, or if journalists were ever used unwittingly as agents. He said Bangladeshi journalists often faced security restrictions in coverage of the gas sector.

I allowed as how, yes, I believed CIA agents sometimes posed as journalists and that journalists were sometimes unwittingly used as agents. I added that the CIA had a tendency to be seen as being everywhere at once much like Allah and that some people at different times in my life had even thought this old rascal to be a CIA agent. There were smiles and laughter all around.

The participant, still smiling, then told me there was a Bangladeshi intelligence agent in the room. I let the conversation drop there, but later asked Mukur who it was. He said it was the course co-ordinator, Sayed Ishtiaque Reza, a senior reporter for *The Financial Express*, who had helped me and BCDJC arrange some of the guest speakers.

Another light moment came when silk entered the conversation. The discussion had turned to the Bangladesh garment sector which is one of the principal earners of foreign currency in the country. I told the gathering that Thailand had just developed a new silk garment for domestic use and export that might be pirated in Bangladesh. It's a bullet proof vest. It reportedly stops .38 caliber bullets, is lightweight and less bulky than the Teflon variety, and sells for $100 as compared to $300. Designed most probably is my conjecture by a notorious American Thai silk tycoon who disappeared some years ago under mysterious circumstances while on a visit to Malaysia. I see a big future for such a garment in Bangladesh among the general public, police, and army.

And so it would be fair to say that this old fart broke some fresh wind in this gas training course.

Gas Pains

1/7/99

Catching up with local and regional news that transpired during the
workshop, there were several stories in the press indicating that law
and order continues to be a problem in the country. In two districts in
the Chittagong Hill Tracts, it was reported that at least five people
have been killed in some 50 recent clashes between supporters of the
1988 peace accord and opponents.

The peace treaty ended a 22-year-old insurgency by the Shanti
Bahini guerrillas in the region, but many tribal people believe the government has not made good on its promises to implement reforms in
the region. Numerous cases of kidnapping, stealing, muggings and
other forms of civil disorder have been reported.

* * *

In Dhaka, a leader of the labor front of the ruling Awami League party was gunned down by several assailants in broad daylight Wednesday as he left a court building for lunch. He later died at the hospital from his gunshot wounds fired at point-blank range. The victim had been scheduled to testify in a case involving the making of explosives.

Meanwhile, the number of terrorists in custody from the nationwide combing operation that began about two months ago now exceeds 50,000. And *The Independent* reported Wednesday that many of them are "living in the lap of luxury." The terrorists, many of whom once worked for the ruling Awami League, are demanding gourmet food, TV and radio, mobile phones, and even soap and water from their custodians. And so the farce continues.

* * *

In a sign of growing labor unrest, rail and road links between Dhaka and Chittagong reopened today as factory workers ended a two-day blockade after receiving assurance their demands for higher wages would be considered in the near future. The blockade near Chittagong stopped delivery of freight from the country's main port. Transport operators said buses and trucks were again using the Dhaka-Chittagong highway to move goods and people stranded since Tuesday. Protesters had ripped up about 300 feet of railroad track.

It was the second protest over wages in two weeks. On June 16, mill workers set up a similar blockade to press authorities to implement the recommendation of a 1991 wage commission to increase their monthly wage to 1,000 taka ($20.62) from 900 taka. The protest had been further fueled by non-payment of salaries for the last six months in three private jute mills.

186

The official rate of inflation in the country is near 9 percent at the moment.

2/7/99

Another nationwide dawn-to-dusk hartal has been called by the opposition for July 8 to protest the budget. Some are angry because it provides for the purchase of eight Russian MIG-29 fighters for $116 million. The deal apparently has already been struck. Washington has refused to sell Bangladesh F-16 fighters. The question, of course, is why does impoverished Bangladesh need such sophisticated aircraft when it faces no threat from its neighbors—India and Burma. Perhaps it wants to use them against the mastans and other terrorists inside Bangladesh.

Flying three minutes in any direction actually would put the MIGs out of Bangladeshi air space.

*　　*　　*

The many moods of monsoon cloud my thoughts today. Four power outages this morning. The humidity fogs my glasses, but not my vision. This is the day the American community here celebrates the 4th of July. I'm not sure why, but it being Friday it is an Islamic holiday anyway. I had a hot dog and a beer at the American Mission Club and was given a T-shirt commemorating the day donated by Unocal, the gas exploration people. I sat poolside under a tarp in the monsoon rain and almost cried when Dixie was played over the flag-draped loudspeakers. Tonight a dinner-dance is scheduled. Bathing suits are optional. I'm laughing and singing in the rain. Not to mention dancing. Cry your heart out Gene Kelly.

*   *   *

Meanwhile, the army has been called out and dispatched to threatened embankments in various towns across the country where flood waters are very near to overflowing and creating fresh disasters. Nineteen dead to date in the southeast and 10 missing in the northern districts with thousands of people displaced and marooned.

*   *   *

Skin and bones. That's the plight of the poor Royal Bengal Tigers at the hands of poachers in the Sundarbans, a UNESCO World Heritage site in the mangrove forests of the southeast. The Forestry Department reports the hunt for the majestic aphrodisiacs has reduced the population to about 360 animals, which is about the number of people they have reportedly eaten over the last three years.

3/7/99

Nayeem has asked me to become a member of his International Advisory Board and to oversee the recruitment of eight to 10 others who would give counsel and advice to BCDJC and lend their authority to the organization. I said I would.

I treated myself to lunch at the Sonagaron Hotel, a five star in the Dhaka galaxy within shooting distance of several black holes. What a shock when the bill came. Eight dollars for a bad glass of wine!

4/7/99

The real 4th of July is at hand. A big party is planned at the US
Embassy for the influential underworld of Bangladesh. I'm not invited. But I did meet the US Marine who is in charge of security at the
Embassy. Sat with him and his wife and a couple of other spit and pol-
ish types at the US Mission Club dinner dance. The black John Wayne
type hails from Savannah, Georgia.

* * *

I mentioned to Nayeem my mild dissatisfaction at learning that a
Bangladeshi intelligence agent had been assigned to be my course co-
coordinator for the workshop on gas development issues. It stacked
the deck in favor of the government position, I argued. He squirmed
a bit, but indicated that he himself and the Centre might have been
the target of investigation rather than the course itself.

He said Sayed Ishtiaque Reza's uncle was a colonel in Army intelligence and that *The Financial Express* senior reporter had a sick wife
and needed additional money to help pay her medical bills. It was not
uncommon for journalists in Bangladesh, Nayeem added, to work for
intelligence agencies—the two main ones being the Army and a joint
military-police organization. He allowed as how many agents were
poorly trained and generally incapable of asking relevant questions.
He then went into a long digression about four incidents where he
had been interrogated for long periods by intelligence agents back in
the early '90's when he was editor of the daily *Ajker Kagoj*.

In one incident, he was hauled before interrogators for three and a
half hours for having visited the offices of the Indian High
Commission. His mission had been to purchase tickets to a concert to

189

be given by a visiting Indian female folk singer. But the intelligence agency suspected something more sinister.

On another occasion, his paper was running out of funds and he approached a wealthy Indian businessman to see if he would be interested in funding the endeavor. This brought a full night of interrogation.

In another incident described, Nayeem printed a story based on a conversation he overheard. Dhaka had been building a rushed embankment around the city to protect it from flooding. The building of the embankment was entrusted in sectors to different organizations—one of them being the Army. A relative, who was a major in the Army, confided to a gathering that Nayeem attended that the Army's workmanship was shoddy.

In still another incident, Nayeem reported on a confidential Army edict that ordered all personnel riding in vehicles in the city to carry arms.

These incidents and others, one imagines, gather dust somewhere in Nayeem's bulky intelligence dossier.

Meanwhile, the political dynamics of all this are interesting. Two key Centre players, Azfar and Mukur, appear to be aligned with the Awami League while Nayeem apparently bends like a reed in the wind which at the moment is prevailing toward the opposition Bangladesh Nationalist Party, but could very well come around at any moment toward the Awami League. Interestingly, it was Azfar who suggested his close friend Reza be course coordinator for the gas workshop. The "game," in Nayeem's word, continues.

5/7/99

Nayeem decided today to pay a 20-day visit to the United States where he will attend a Kettering Foundation workshop on promoting democracy at the grassroots level. He plans to visit the International Center for Journalists in Washington, DC, on July 14. On the way, he will stop off in Cardiff, Wales, for a meeting with the Thomson Foundation people. He leaves July 8.

6/7/99

Supporters of an alleged gangland mobster went on the rampage in Chittagong today to protest against the arrest of their leader. Police reported the rampage began after word of the arrest of Mohammad Nasir at a hideout here in Dhaka. Angry followers damaged at least 100 cars, fired shots in the air, and exploded bombs, creating a reign of terror. Police said they had no reports of casualties.

Delivery of cargo from the port was disrupted and buses withdrew from the roads, stranding thousands of passengers. The protesters demanded the immediate release of Nasir, a Chittagong leader of the ruling Awami League who was expelled from the party recently on charges of criminal activities. Nasir was wanted by police on several charges, including murder.

Met with Val Williams of the Thomson Foundation. He is in charge of finances,

The Media

7/7/99

In the course of my training rounds, I have often been asked what I think about the press in Bangladesh. It is not an easy question to answer. There are really two presses in Bangladesh, one for the English-speaking elite and another for the literate Bangla-reading population. Neither press is read by the vast majority of the 126 or so million people in the country. This is particularly true at the grassroots level where many of the people are illiterate.

While on the surface the press, which has a total readership of 2.2 million people, appears to enjoy freedom to express a wide variety of views, in reality it is severely restricted by a lack of transparency and accountability on the part of the government and hampered by a social malaise where corruption is endemic to the system and many reporters are little more than public relations vehicles for vested interests.

"The history of Bangladesh since its independence (in 1971), merely reconfirms that a lack of participation on the part of the people has not only deterred the progress of the country, but has also made the society more corrupt and vulnerable to terror and prejudice." These were the words of a lawyer, Amir-ul Islam, who attended an international conference in early July in Dhaka on the "Right to Information."

It has been clear to me in my discussions with countless professional Bangladeshi journalists that they are frustrated by their lack of access to government ministries and records. This despite Article 39 of the Constitution which guarantees press freedoms as part of freedom of expression and the establishment of a Press Council to prevent abuse of freedom of the press.

There is a substantial difference between what Bangla newspapers print and the material in the English-language press, according to Nayeem Islam Khan, executive director of the Bangladesh Centre for Development, Journalism and Communication. The English-language press, he said, caters to an elite, generally highly educated audience which serves in most cases the interests of the foreign community. In general, the reporting is of a higher caliber in terms of accuracy, but still many errors creep in. The politics are more subtle, more sophisticated, and biases are thinly disguised. The reporters, of course, are more highly paid.

In the Bangla press, the stories are more 'biting', more interesting generally, but the facts, even simple ones, are always suspect. For example, the Prime Minister was presented a bouquet by a student group while leading a procession in the streets. Twelve Bangla newspapers had the presentation occurring at different locations in the city,

Some Bangla newspapers pay their reporters a living wage, but most do not. Survival thus depends on becoming a PR man for some interest or another. Often this revenue source is shared with the newspaper. Only bureau chiefs are generally paid outside Dhaka and there are not too many of those. As a general rule, correspondents in the field are not paid, thus stories from the countryside serve the interests of those who pay the reporters for coverage of an event or the reporter's own interest.

According to Ministry of Foreign Affairs 1998 figures, there are 284 daily newspapers in the country. Of these, five—*The Daily Star, The Daily Observer, The Independent, The New Nation,* and *The Financial Express*—are the main Dhaka-based English-language publications. The total English-language circulation in Dhaka was 168,210 with 19,502 from papers elsewhere, mainly Chittagong. The combined circulation of all daily newspapers was 2.2 million.

Four Bangla daily newspapers of note are the Muktakantha, the Manavzamin, Ittefaq, and the Janakantha. The total circulation of Bangla newspapers is 2,055,640.

The daily newspapers subscribe to two local news agencies—Associated Press of Bangladesh and United News of Bangladesh—plus two foreign agencies—Agence France Press and Reuters. There is also the state-run Bangladesh Sangbad Sangstha.

Reuters and the Associated Press are staffed entirely by Bangladesh nationals which tends to give a distorted and highly selective view of what is happening in the country. In a sense, I believe this to be a form of censorship and control over news leaving the country.

It is generally believed that Bangladesh has reached its saturation point in the publication of daily newspapers. Many of the daily papers are four-page affairs representing a particular political point of view. They come and go with regular frequency.

There are plans to privatize Bangladesh Television (BTV). It has two stations in Dhaka, and two in Chittagong, and 11 relay stations around the country.

State-owned Bangladesh Betar (Radio) has a countrywide network with 10 regional stations.

It is thus obvious that the government still controls the media reaching the majority of the people in the country and only pays lip service to the free flow of information.

8/7/99

One policeman was killed and eleven others injured in a series of bomb attacks in Dhaka last night in pre-hartal violence. Police believed the bomb blasts were the work of opposition activists ahead of the nationwide strike today.

A police spokesman said the bombs were homemade. About fifteen to twenty bombs exploded within a few minutes of each other. An additional four people were injured. There were no arrests. *The Daily Star* reported that a special police detachment to contain riots went on a rampage after learning that one of their comrades had been killed, damaging several vehicles in the area.

Schools, shops, factories and private offices were shut today across the country and transportation was at a standstill in an opposition-led strike fueled in part by rising prices.

In the capital and in Chittagong, extra soldiers and police were called out to help maintain security. One man was killed and hundreds wounded during clashes in a similar strike on June 13.

An alliance of major opposition parties, led by former prime minister Begum Khaleda Zia of the Bangladesh Nationalist Party, called the strike to protest over what they termed an "anti-people budget" and other concerns, including deteriorating law and order and "soaring" prices of essential commodities. Inflation is officially running at 8.8 percent.

A BNP spokesman said the strike was also intended to protest "a conspiracy by the government" to sell natural gas to India, which opposition parties say would drain Bangladesh of a major resource. Prime Minister Sheikh Hasina has repeatedly said Bangladesh has no plans to export gas in the near future.

9/7/99

While the cat's away, the mice will play. Prime Minister Sheikh Hasina was in London yesterday on a state visit as bomb blasts in downtown Dhaka continued for a second straight day yesterday. An anti-government dawn-to-dusk hartal forced the closing of schools and businesses and halted traffic across Bangladesh. The strike came a day after violent clashes the night before left one police officer dead and 11 others injured.

Another strike associated death occurred yesterday, raising the death toll to two. Estimates of those injured ranged from 30 to more than 100. Business leaders said the one-day strike cost Bangladesh the equivalent of $68 million in lost production and exports.

Despite the arrests of more than 50,000 suspected terrorists nation-wide, the papers are daily carrying reports from various towns across the country that the law and order situation is deteriorating.

10/7/99

Two were killed and some 700 injured yesterday, 30 critically, in a garment factory fire at Gazipur, a suburb of Dhaka. The fire broke out on the ground floor of the six-story building and many workers elected to jump out of the building. There were no fire exits or escape ladders.

* * *

The recent talk John Kincannon gave at my Workshop on Gas Development Issues, in which he distributed copies in Bangla and English, found its way into a Reuters dispatch yesterday. The dispatch follows:

DHAKA, July 9 (Reuters) - The United States has said Bangladesh could achieve spectacular economic growth rates if it exported natural gas, a move the government and opposition have both opposed.

"No gas company wanted to drill holes to discover gas which they could not bring to market," John Kincannon, director of the U.S. Information Service (USIS) in Bangladesh, told a recent energy seminar.

A copy of his speech was seen by Reuters on Friday.

"If Bangladesh uses gas both in its own right and as an economic multiplier to stimulate investment in export-oriented and domestic industries, there should be no difficulty in boosting economic growth to seven to nine percent," Kincannon said.

Finance Minister S.A.M.S. Kibria has put the country's gross domestic product growth at 5.2 percent in 1998-99 (July-June), which the opposition says is inflated.

Opposition parties oppose gas exports because they fear it would drain the country's only major resource. The government has held back amid uncertainty over the actual size of recoverable reserves, energy officials said.

Prime Minister Sheikh Hasina has said she would prefer to use gas to run gas-based industries before contemplating export.

"In the press, I frequently see the figure that Bangladesh has thirty five years of proven reserves. And then writers go on to conclude that Bangladesh will then run out of gas in 2034," Kincannon said.

"Canada's proven natural gas reserve to production ratio is 12 years, Norway's is 32 years, the Netherlands' is 26 years, and Indonesia's is 30 years — and all of these countries are major gas exporters," he said.

Based on statistics available at Petrobangla, the lone state-owned gas exploration company, Bangladesh has already discovered about 21 trillion cubic feet (tcf) of natural gas, of which around 12.6 tcf can be produced and used for the nation's benefit.

So far, Bangladesh has used about three tcf of this amount, Kincannon said.

"In addition, ongoing exploration has discovered at least five to six tcf in new recoverable reserves. At current rates of consumption, that is roughly 30-35 years worth of proven reserves," Kincannon said.

He said Petrobangla uses a very conservative methodology.

* * *

I start a five-day course in basic journalism for non-professionals tomorrow at the new School of Communications of BCDJC in Dhiamondi.

I met with Arnold Zeitlin, a former Knight Fellow and now Director of the Freedom Forum Center in Hong Kong, at the National Press Club. Arnold is looking to recruit journalists with an interest in Freedom Forum programs. He is also looking for organizations to support Freedom Forum workshops, such as BCDJC, which can offer training facilities and trainers. He said his intentions were to support more programs in Bangladesh, India, and Pakistan.

Had a pizza and beer dinner with Val Williams of the Thomson Foundation. We are both old Reuters hands and know many of the same people. Several Thomson people were sent to China by Val during the years I was there ('93-'94). Also Arnold and I seem to have a number of mutual acquaintances in China.

Monsoon Moods

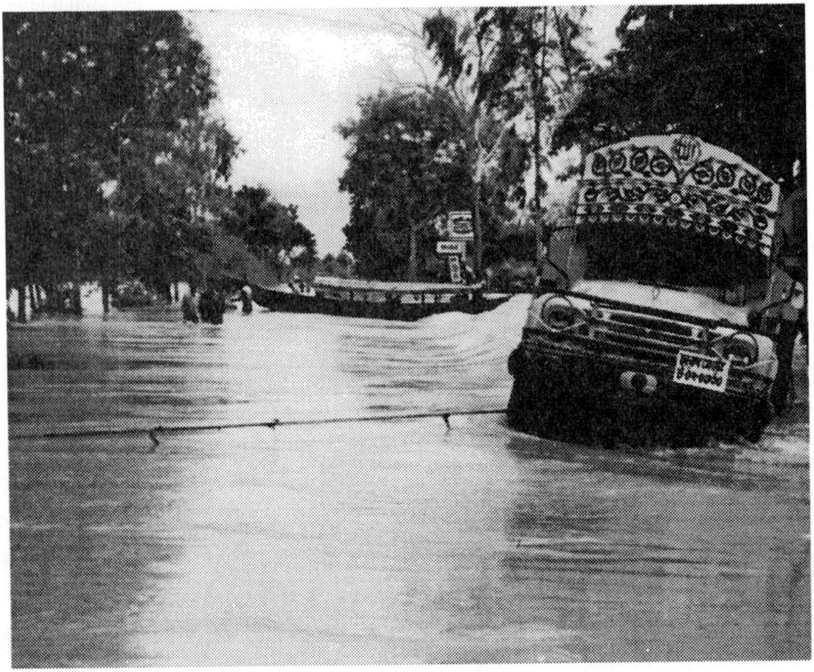

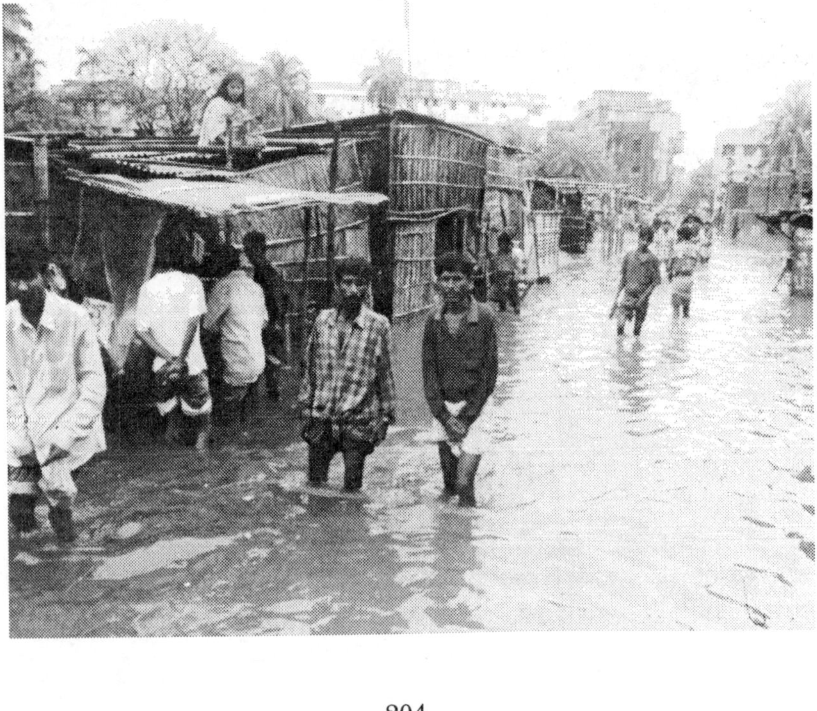

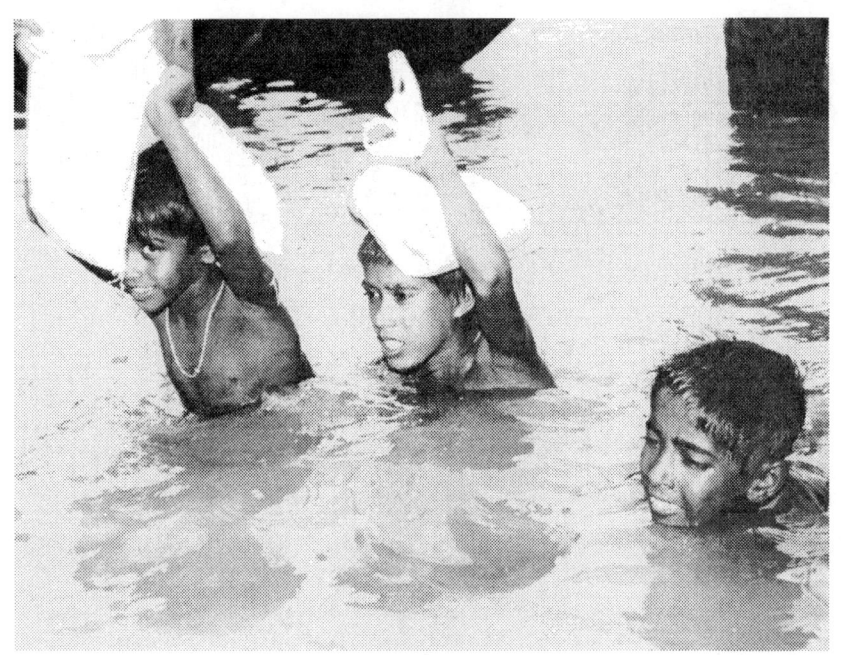

11-15/7/99

Despite more than half a foot of water at the door on opening day, 19 participants turned up, some of them barefoot and with their trousers rolled, for my Basic Journalism Course at BCDJC's new School of Communications. Torrential monsoon rains had everyone worried about whether the Dhaka embankments that surround the city would hold. In fact, they were breached at a few points. In some cars, water was up to the steering wheel.

In the town of Comilla, some three hours distant by car from Dhaka, the warning came in the dead of night. Mosque loudspeakers that usually call Muslims to prayer suddenly blared a command to wake up. The mighty Gumti River had breached its embankment nearby and a raging torrent of water was pouring through the huge hole and flooding the region.

The river flood-waters inundated 110 villages at dawn on Monday and by Thursday there had been reports of 17 deaths, including two children who drowned Tuesday in the swirling waters.

In addition to the Gumti, nine other rivers have breached their embankments in the last month of torrential rains. The rivers have flooded 10 percent of the nation, according to the Flood Forecast Center in Dhaka.

Of the people who live along the Gumti, nearly 50,000 had been evacuated by Wednesday. Another 250,000 people were still marooned, many huddled on the tiny tin roofs of their houses, waiting for relief boats which were few in number because the embankment in this region had not been seriously breached for many years.

Soldiers, civil engineers and volunteers reportedly were fighting a losing battle Wednesday to shore up the embankment with rocks and sandbags. The rupture that in the beginning had been estimated at 130 feet by Wednesday was more than 400 feet in length.

The 100-mile mud embankment had protected hundreds of villages and rice crops from the Gumti River for nearly 30 years. The river runs from the neighboring Indian state of Assam through the Bangladesh delta to the Bay of Bengal.

Breaches, they say, occur almost every year. But in three decades, none has been as great as this breach.

Crisscrossed by 230 rivers, Bangladesh has built more than 5,000 miles of mud embankments to protect villages and crops. While the embankments have helped boost rice production, critics say the floods become more devastating when the levees collapse under pressure.

Last year, floods killed 1,500 people, swamped much of the country and destroyed 2 million tons of rice.

The flooding in Comilla put me in a quandary. It prompted me to send an e-mail to Susan Talalay at the International Center for Journalists in Washington, DC. Susan, and her staff colleagues, are the support team for Knight Fellows in the field.

Dear Susan,

It is my understanding that you may be meeting with Nayeem today (Wednesday). I don't know how well informed he is about events back in Bangladesh. It is my understanding that Mukur and Azfar, his two chief lieutenants, have not told him of the following situation because they don't want to alarm him or worry him unduly while he his on his business in the United States. And to a certain extent I think Bangladeshis have become blasé when it comes to flooding. In any event, if it was me, I'd want to know. The day before yesterday a "huge" part of the Gumti embankment gave way and flooded Comilla, Debidwar, and many surrounding villages. This is the area Nayeem calls home. I believe his family has a house in Comilla. And when I went to give a talk to journalists in Debidwar we visited his family village. Azfar also hails from this area and yesterday reported there was more than a foot of water in his family house, no electricity, and, ironically, no drinking water as the pump was out of commission. Today the papers reported that thousands of people in the area were marooned; that it was the worst flooding in recent memory; that army rescue efforts were hampered by impassable roads where water was waist deep or higher; that efforts to plug the embankment breech had been unsuccessful, and that new ruptures were occurring at other nearby points along the ten-foot embankment. As I understand it, Comilla is not an area that has suffered from severe flooding in the past. Also, there is a second embankment that is supposed to ring the city and protect it from flooding. Also, both Nayeem's and Azfar's family homes, I'm told, are multi-storied buildings. Do with it what you will.

Best regards, Paul

∗   ∗   ∗

The Basic Journalism Course for non-professionals was a hit. On Wednesday evening we held a "cultural event." Professional singers and musicians, gathered by my Bangla teacher Rupa who is also a local TV personality, were brought in. A stage was erected. Various performers, including a couple of class participants, read poetry. Olivier paled by comparison to my rendition of Hamlet's "To be, or not to be" soliloquy, followed by a raging poem by Dylan Thomas, and then one of my own, to appropriately enough, as it was raining outside, thunderous applause. The one and a half hour program was followed by tea and bananas.

The caliber of workshop participants, in my opinion, was much higher than previous workshops where I have taught professional journalists. Their writing exercises—all in English—led me to conclude that most of them could find work at a mid-career level on a Bangladesh newspaper. Nearly half of the 19 participants were women,

On the final day (Thursday), one of the women participants was mugged close to the school while on the way to class. She lost a necklace valued at about $100. Three men in a motorized "baby taxi" cut off her rickshaw and one of them held a knife to her throat and demanded her valuables.

There was much debate over whether the incident should be reported to the police. I insisted that she do so and one of the school aides accompanied her to the police station.

16/7/99

There are an estimated 30,000 prostitutes in Bangladesh and hundreds of them yesterday refused to sign a pledge to give up the oldest profession despite a government promise to help provide them alternate careers.

Prime Minister Sheikh Hasina's government has launched a $4.1 million program that promises jobs and small businesses to the sex workers. But there were few takers Friday.

Officials from the state-run Social Welfare Department on Thursday visited the century-old Tanbazar brothel, the country's largest and oldest red light district.

The district is in the river-front town of Narayanganj near, Dhaka. They tried to get the some 3,000 prostitutes residing there to sign documents making them eligible for loans: 736 signed. A predominantly Muslim nation, Bangladesh clerics frown on prostitution. Still, a woman is free to register as a prostitute if a magistrate certifies that this is the only way she can survive.

It was the third government attempt to persuade prostitutes to rehabilitate. The previous ones in 1985 and 1989 failed. Among those who had accepted previous offers, many returned to prostitution when faced with social rejection.

Last week, a group of clerics visited Tanbazar, a row of flimsy tin sheds and dilapidated buildings. They asked the women to repent for their sins and ask for Allah's forgiveness."

A few laughed openly at the clerics.

17/7/99

The flooding in Comilla and the surrounding area continued to be
serious yesterday as the level of the Gumti river fell slightly below the
danger level, but three large breeches in the embankment allowed
water to continue to pour into the region, Some 70,000 people were
displaced. A bridge in the area collapsed closing the road to Sylhet.
And the Dhaka-Chittagong highway had a stretch of about 100 feet
where the water was about a foot deep but still passable, if slowly. The
roadbed is considered high ground in this area. The Gumti flows
down from the Himalayas where there has been considerable rain of
late. Fortunately, the monsoon rains have not fallen heavily in the
Comilla area since last Tuesday.

*　　*　　*

On the subject of highways, the World Bank reported this week that
more than 5,000 people every year are killed in road accidents in
Bangladesh. My heart is in my throat every time I climb into a car
here.

*　　*　　*

Another statistical gem: The police report that despite the present
crackdown on terrorists and criminals, the number of crimes committed in the first five months of the year compared to the same period
last year rose substantially. The figures are: 1,571 murdered, 490 kid-
napped, 1,264 raped, and 53 victims of acid attacks. Because many

people do not report crimes, it is a safe assumption that these figures are most probably much higher.

18/7/99

There are not too many success stories in Bangladesh, but the Grameen Bank is one of them. Dr. Mohammad Eunus, once an economics professor at Chittagong University, started the Grameen Bank in 1983. It is still going strong. Of the top 20 micro credit institutions in the world, Grameen ranks number two. By the end of 1996, the last year for which figures are available here, the bank had distributed more than $1.7 billion in loans and had a better than 95 percent recovery rate. The total saving of members is in excess of $125 million. It has provided loans to 1.2 million members, 94 percent of whom are women. Since collateral is not required for a loan and the credit programs target the rural poor, the group mechanism is used to ensure repayment.

Groups are formed by individuals themselves (men and women). There are usually five to a group. Loans are disbursed to members only with the approval of the group. A 1998 survey found Grameen members to have a 28 percent higher income rate than non-borrowers.

Six or eight groups often ban together to form a center within a given village. The center meets once a week to discuss loan applications.

The John F. Kennedy Jr. story has flooded my TV with pictures of the Cape in summer and Woods Hole in particular. I even think I got a glimpse of my younger son Michael out in his rescue vessel Sea Tow. I'm very familiar with the Gay Head area and have fished the waters off No Man's Land, Menemsha, and Cuttyhunk often for striped bass. The waters are full of 5-6 foot blue sharks, which will attack humans. One suspects his plane suffered a mechanical failure like a snapped cable, or that he experienced a heart attack, or possibly he was the victim of foul play. Sad! I still remember the day I shook JFK's hand, in 1960 I think it was, when he came campaigning into the newsroom of the Quincy Patriot Ledger where I was working as news editor. And Ted Kennedy's youngest son Teddy Jr., who lost a leg to cancer, and I, sailed together and played on the Woods Hole Oceanographic Institution's Marine Policy softball team in the late '80s. I was 7-2 my last year as pitcher.

Coincidentally, I ran into James Ostergard at lunch at the American Mission Club. Jim was formerly Master of the Chain, Atlantis, and other vessels at the Woods Hole Oceanographic Institution, where I worked for 13 years as Editor of Oceanus, a magazine of marine science and policy. He is here in Bangladesh as an adviser to some American shrimp processors. We talked of mutual acquaintances, including Dick Bachus, the authority on Georges Bank. Jim wrote a chapter for Dick's definitive book on the Bank from the fisherman's perspective.

19/7/99

I fixed two more workshops today, one another basic course for non-professionals from July 31 to 2 August, and an environmentally focused workshop for professionals on the Sundarbans from 8 to 10 August.

* * *

Azfar, back from Comilla, reports that the danger there has subsided. The Gumti River, it seems, all on its own, has divided below Comilla to form two rivers which has released a lot of the pressure.

* * *

Bangladesh has devalued the taka about 2 percent to try to boost exports. The devaluation, the first in the current fiscal year, became effective July 15. One dollar is now worth 49.50 taka. The old rate was 48.50. The last devaluation was in October 1998.

20/7/99

As this journal attests to, political violence is a way of life in Bangladesh. It is my contention that this is one of the major factors that could one day in the not too distant future plunge the country into civil war. Take the case of Feni, where this week two people were gunned down. Over the last three years, political violence there has left at least 60 dead and 300 injured, according to police reports.

The latest victims of the southeastern town's lethal feud between the ruling Awami League and opposition Bangladesh Nationalist Party (BNP) died on July 20 in an exchange of gunfire.

Violence and loss of lives have become a routine feature in the town with no end in sight. The two victims were Awami activist Omar Faruk, 18, and an unidentified rickshaw-puller.

Gunmen from the Awami League, headed by Prime Minister Sheikh Hasina, and the opposition BNP, led by former prime minister Begum Khaleda Zia, have launched a reign of terror.

The rival groups have taken hostages and tortured people for money in bids to assert influence and control over the town. "BNP terrorists have killed 24 leaders and workers of our party in the last three years," said Zainal Hazari, an Awami Member of Parliament from Feni, which is 118 miles from Dhaka.

Local BNP leader Zainul Abedin said: "Awami gunmen have shot and killed at least 17 of our people here since 1996." Both leaders were quoted as having made their remarks in a Reuters dispatch. At least 19 others have died in shootouts between the two groups.

"The situation is beyond our control. The rival political activists use more sophisticated weapons and are blessed by their central leadership," Police Inspector Abdur Rashid was quoted as having said.

*　　*　　*

The monsoon season is heading into its most dangerous phase. Many rivers across the land are running above the danger level and the next couple of weeks will see how much of the country goes under water. Two more days of torrential rains this week have flooded another 10 villages in northern Bangladesh, marooning at least 20,000 people.

Rescue teams have been dispatched with food and medicine after the Padma and Jamuna rivers rose above danger levels in an area about 65 miles north of Dhaka.

Last week, some 55,000 people were forced out of their homes when the Gumti overflowed its dirt embankment and submerged 200 villages in the Comilla district, 55 miles east of Dhaka. Most of these people are now camped on the river embankment.

Another 250,000 people were hit by the floods in Comilla after army troops and civil engineers failed to plug a 700-foot breach in the Gumti levee. Two more mud levees collapsed in Laxmipur district in eastern Bangladesh over the weekend.

Nineteen people have been killed by floods so far during this monsoon season.

21/7/99

Another Bangla lesson. My fluency is now greater than that of a fine parrot. Colorful phases flow from my mouth with glacial frequency. I think I'm ready for a major role in a silent movie which are just being made here.

*   *   *

Met with Hasan Mansur, the founder and managing director of The Guide, the major tour agency here specializing in eco-tourism trips into the Sundarbans. In more than 150 trips into the Sundarbans, Hasan has seen only one tiger. But his son, a photographer, has seen many and recently got some excellent footage which will air on the Discovery channel in October. Hasan and his son will be guest speakers on August 10 during my workshop on the Sundarbans. He provided me with some good material on the fauna and flora in the region.

The Guide operates two tour vessels into the Sundarbans, one capable of handling 50 passengers and another smaller vessel with a capacity for 24 individuals.

22/7/99

An earthquake jolted the southern coast of Bangladesh today, leaving at least six dead and 500 injured. The intensity of the quake on Maheskhali, which is an island of about 50 square miles, and in the neighboring coastal areas was recorded as between 4.7 and 5.2 on the Richter scale. The island is located about 60 miles south of Chittagong.

Maheskhali is home to some 250,000 people, mainly fisherfolk. It is 18 miles off the coast of Cox's Bazar, a resort town known for its long beach, smuggling, and lack of tourism. The quake lasted up to one minute. The tremors were also felt in Cox's Bazar. The island is 185 miles south of Dhaka.

Bangladesh is in a major seismic zone and has experienced seven earthquakes of 7 or more points magnitude on the Richter scale, the greatest being in 1897 and reconstructed at 8.7. A major earthquake in Dhaka is considered just another disaster waiting to happen.

23/7/99

The top 5 percent of the population in Dhaka are getting richer while the poor, you guessed it, are getting poorer despite earning more money. Incomes for slum dwellers have risen to $250 a year from $165 in 1991, according to an International Rice Research Institute study.

Dhaka has a population of close to 10 million which is projected to be 19 million by 2020.

*　*　*

Members of Parliament owe the government huge sums of money for unpaid telephone and fax bills despite the fact they receive an $80 per month allowance from the treasury. Some of the bills go back 20 years. If an ordinary Bangladeshi defaults on his bill for more than two months, he/she is cut off. The telephone company does not dare cut the MPs off for fear of violent retaliation.

*　*　*

The opposition has scheduled another three-day road march, starting July 25. Bring your umbrella.

*　*　*

My driver was in tears. Nayeem's car was run into by a Tempo bus, a larger version of the "baby taxi," on the way to pick me up, doing serious damage to the rear right hand door. Will Nayeem try to get the price of repair out of me? He has no collision insurance on the car. The Tempo fled the scene.

24/7/99

I'm bracing for the final bill from Nayeem. At the moment, $500 is in dispute. When Mukur gave me my car bill for the first three months, he overcharged me $100 per month for the rental, or $600. I argued with Nayeem and he reduced it to the amount we had agreed on, $500 a month. I was also charged $200 a month for gas and oil, which is outrageous. I don't use the car that much and for the first three months I was out of Dhaka for at least a week each month. Mukur was

217

trying to get me to pay for the Centre's use of the car. I said I would pay $100 a month, but no more. So that is $300 of the amount in dispute. Then, I contend I gave $200 to Mukur toward my Bangla lessons. He maintains he has no recollection or record of such a payment. I have a slip of paper indicating I did pay the amount. When I first arrived, I arranged a rental car for myself, but Nayeem saw an opportunity for some income and offered me one of his two cars and a driver at the same rate I was paying to the car rental agency. I agreed.

As a rule of thumb, the Muslim culture in Bangladesh dictates that foreigners, particularly those here on humanitarian missions, should pay double for any service rendered. The attitude is one of "we are going to make you pay for the humiliation of our colonial legacy and the arrogance that springs from believing you are superior to us." Bangladeshis are rapacious traders who will exploit the slightest sign of weakness. It's sort of a tax on having been forced to beg for existence. And, in my mind, an unpleasant one.

✳   ✳   ✳

Nayeem today sent an e-mail requesting that I extend by departure by 15 to 20 days to help him with administrative details connected with his "very successful" US trip and a UNDP Asian peace conference he is bidding to manage the first week in September. Some 250 top Asian parliamentarians are expected in town for the latter event and the UNDP wants wall-to-wall press coverage as well as red carpet treatment. The deadline for bids is July 29 at 4 pm.

218

25/7/99

Main opposition leader Begum Khaleda Zia, the former prime minister, left Dhaka in a white jeep today, accompanied by a convoy of some
500 vehicles which will reach the town of Mymensingh, 200 miles
north on Tuesday. She is scheduled to address at least 25 roadside rallies along the way to whip up support for her campaign to oust the
government under the banner of her Bangladesh Nationalist Party
(BNP).

Khaleda told some 15,000 supporters at Mawna, 40 miles from the
capital, the main slogan of her campaign was "remove (ruling) Awami
League and save Bangladesh." Khaleda accused her successor, prime
minister Sheikh Hasina, of "perpetuating a dreaded misrule that has
tarnished the country's democratic image and caused immense suffer-
ings to the people."

Bangladesh's former president, Hossain Mohammad Ershad, leader
of the opposition Jatiya Party, meanwhile, set out on a three-day boat
trip to southern coastal districts to promote the same cause. Ershad's
motor launch was accompanied by several vessels.

The BNP's other partners, the fundamentalist Jamaat-e-Islami party
and Islami Oikyo Jote, took different road routes. The road and boat
actions are widely seen as alternative agitations to bloody nationwide
hartals. A similar road march in May passed peacefully with some
political analysts calling the tactic, while non-violent, a failure.

26/7/99

Nayeem returns tomorrow morning from his trip to the United States. There is a flurry of activity at the Centre to make things ready for his return. The damaged car door has been hammered out, but still needs a paint job. Mukur and Azfar are busy with calculating the bids for the UNDP peace conference. We have 12 participants committed for my Basic Journalism Workshop beginning on the 31st of July, but only four so far for the environmental course on the Sundarbans, to begin on August 9th. My Bangla class was cancelled. My last Bangla class is on the 28th.

It has turned very hot and humid again. Monsoon rains, although forecast, have left only dried tears on the cheeks of my day.

27/7/99

Unocal Corporation, the California-based oil and gas multinational exploration giant, now owns Bangladesh. On Monday it acquired three prime gas blocks covering nearly 3.4 acres in northeastern Bangladesh from Occidental Petroleum Corporation.

Occidental, a pioneer investor in Bangladesh's gas sector since 1995 and also an American corporation, acquired three oil fields from Unocal in Yemen under the deal.

Unocal's investment in Bangladesh totals $260 million. It inherited liabilities worth $125 million for environmental damage caused by a 1997 gas field fire that started during drilling by Occidental.

Unocal is based in El Segundo, California. Occidental is based in Los Angeles.

Bangladesh's main natural resource is gas. There is a heated national debate at the moment over whether to export the resource, for which there is no accurate public assessment of the amount, but it is speculated to be huge. Both the present Awami League government and the Bangladesh Nationalist Party-led opposition coalition are against export, which in essence means to India via pipeline because the country cannot afford Liquid Natural Gas tankers and the associated facilities needed for this type of transport. Bangladesh's neighbor Burma has said it would be willing to supply gas to India via pipeline over Bangladesh territory should one be built. Unocal already ships gas to Thailand via a very controversially constructed pipeline from Burma. Bangladesh wants to use its gas domestically for industrial, energy, and home purposes.

*   *   *

Violence reared its ugly head on the campaign trail yesterday. Seven are dead and at least 50 injured. Two died when a bus carrying Jamaat party leaders and activists hit a rickshaw and crushed the driver and passenger at Pabna. Another died when a minivan, also carrying Jamaat activists, hit and killed an eight-year-old boy on the road. The deaths sparked clashes between opposition activists and local villagers armed with sticks and wooden spears.

Also yesterday, a truck rammed into the BNP motorcade, and then ploughed into a crowd that had gathered to watch the parade.

Four people died in that crash, near Sherpur, 160 miles north of Dhaka. The Fundamentalist Jamaat convoy is headed by party leader Golam Azam.

*   *   *

We all know the oldest profession is a tough business. It has gotten even tougher this week in Bangladesh. Early on July 24, police raided the Tanbazar red-light district near Dhaka after more than 2,000 women refused to quit prostitution and take government-sponsored jobs. About 300 of the women were taken to Kasimpur, a state complex surrounded by 10-foot-high walls and barbed wire, 20 miles north of here.

Yesterday, the prostitutes who were placed in the state-run home for destitute women went on a hunger strike after clashes with police and staff members.

Angry prostitutes, reportedly armed with firewood and bricks, smashed windows at the center and attacked police, according to eyewitnesses. Police and staff reportedly kicked and beat the protesters.

The violence left at least 50 people injured, most of them prostitutes. "We heard the women screaming and saw police beating them with batons," one local farmer was quoted by the Associated Press as having said. Guards refused to allow journalists into the complex.

Three prostitutes climbed a tree inside the complex today, and shouted to reporters outside that they had stopped eating and drinking in protest. "We want to get out of this hell," one of them yelled. The women were soon grabbed by security forces.

Dozens of Bangladeshi human rights groups have denounced the eviction of the prostitutes, all of whom were legally registered to work in the sex trade.

What Life is All About
According to my e-mail

Life is about who you love and who you hurt.
It's about who you make happy or unhappy purposefully.
It's about keeping or betraying trust. It's about friendship, used as
a sanctity or a weapon.
It's about what you say and mean, maybe hurtful, maybe hearten-
ing.
It's about starting rumors and contributing to petty gossip.
It's about what judgments you
pass and why. And who your judgments are spread to.
It's about who you've ignored with full control and intention.
It's about jealousy, fear, ignorance, and revenge.
It's about carrying inner hate
and love, letting it grow, and spreading it.
But most of all, it's about using your life to touch or poison the
people's hearts in such a way that could have never occurred alone.
Only you choose the way those hearts are affected, and those choic-
es are what life's all about.

29/7/99

Nayeem has returned from the United States with a photo album full
of pictures of himself with his arm around a bevy of attractive, smiling

women he met while on tour. I understand he had to sedate his young wife before showing her the album.

Nayeem wants me, before my departure, to help him draft two proposals for the Media Development Loan Fund in connection with the newspaper he is seeking to launch. He was very upbeat about his trip, the Kettering seminar, and the contacts he made in the US.

It turns out that Nayeem's family home in Comilla did experience serious flooding, but his family village, though marooned for several days, escaped the deluge because it occupied relatively high ground. The surrounding villages and roads, however, went underwater.

The flooding in Comilla has caused the deaths of at least two people living in shelters which in turn has sparked widespread protests in the town today, resulting in a barricade of roads in the areas, stranding some 5,000 vehicles. The protesters are demanding food aid.

Nayeem is not enthusiastic about bidding on the UNDP peace conference. Too political, he thinks. It is unclear to me whether he even bid for the work.

* * *

I witnessed another incident of police brutality on my way to the office today. Stopped in heavy traffic at a roundabout, I saw a policeman ahead in a fit of rage take off his plastic helmet and indiscriminately start hitting passing rickshaw drivers and their passengers about the head and body, Apparently he was incensed that they had not stopped at the circle.

* * *

The opposition has called a 30-hour hartal to begin at 6 am on August 2 in protest of a government decision to allow transshipment of goods from India across Bangladesh to other parts of India. This could wipeout the final day of my Basic Journalism Workshop which begins on the 31st. It also could be an extremely bloody hartal given the nationalistic passions aroused over the issue.

*　　*　　*

The Independent has reported that "economic terrorists" with "high connections" have flooded the market with bogus currency, mainly 500 and 100 taka notes, which, of course, are the denominations I mostly carry. Apparently the forgers are working out of India and the quality of the bogus notes are reportedly very good.

*　　*　　*

In more political violence, two rival groups of government Secretariat employees clashed in downtown Dhaka today for more than three hours over pay and other demands. The police resorted to tear gas and baton charges to disperse the groups. Some 30, including several policemen, were injured.

30/7/99

Major national power outage forecast for today.

*　　*　　*

Preparing for Basic Journalism Workshop which opens tomorrow at Centre's new School of Communications in Dhiamondi.

31/7/99

The sex workers saga reached a bloody climax this week when at least 50 women were injured in a stampede after unidentified gunmen opened fire on the protesting workers and women's rights activists near Dhaka.

The incident occurred yesterday during a rally to protest the forced eviction of thousands of prostitutes from the 111-year-old "red-light" district in Narayanganj, a town some12 miles from Dhaka.

The gunmen fired several shots from automatic weapons apparently trying to disperse the rally. No one was killed or injured by gunfire, but the sound of the shooting set off a stampede. The gunmen fled before the police arrived. The rally in Narayanganj's Tanbazar area was organized by Sanghati — a forum of 59 women organizations.

The brothel housed some 3,500 legally licensed prostitutes. It was shut down last Saturday under pressure from civil and religious groups. .

At the brothel site on Friday, Muslim mullahs held special prayers to "cleanse" the district.

About 300 women who lived in the brothel were detained earlier in the week by police and sent to a grim state facility for destitute women in Kashimpur, north of Dhaka.

*   *   *

Twelve participants turned up for my Basic Journalism Workshop which went off smoothly. Because a 30-hour hartal has been called on the last scheduled day of the course, it was voted to hold the final day on the 6th of August or the next formal day of prayer. The weather is hot, hot, hot, and humid.It rains but once or twice a day.

1/8/99

Another day of class. Three and a half hours of lecturing with occasional breaks for tea. This is a one-man show. The participants are rather docile, but attentive. Thank Allah for air-conditioning.

2/8/99

A 30-hour Hartal began at 6 am. Pre-hartal violence was minimal. Opposition activists marched in the streets of downtown Dhaka last night and set off a number of home made bombs, but only six people were reported injured and there apparently were no deaths. But the situation everywhere is very tense. Nayeem traveled by rickshaw to my guest house this morning (a journey of about 8 miles) and reported the roads were nearly empty and most shops closed. We discussed the new newspaper he wants to launch and the proposal to the Media Development Loan Fund I'm helping him draft.

Thousands of riot police have been deployed here in the capital and elsewhere across the country. Tension is high in border areas with India, on university campuses, and among port workers, and government employees, particularly those working at the Secretariat where they went on a rampage yesterday ransacking several offices. The flashpoint will most likely occur later tonight under the cover of darkness.

3/8/99

The 30-hour hartal strike was over at noon today. At least 60 people have been injured in clashes between police and opposition activists in downtown Dhaka and elsewhere during the action. The government says it has agreed in principle to allow Indian goods to be transported across the country using Bangladeshi trucks, a deal that could earn Bangladesh $400 million a year. India needs the transport route to supply its isolated northeast states.

Commerce and Industry Minister Tofael Ahmed says a formal deal has yet to be signed.

The opposition, meanwhile, threatened a non-stop hartal if the government did not stop the deal with India. As it was, they announced a month-long series of "agitations" to begin on August 7.

The 30-hour suffocating hartal disrupted transportation and business across the country and caused a great deal of general misery not to mention the loss of untold millions of dollars in lost productivity.

❋ ❋ ❋

Three muggers faced mob justice shortly after the hartal came to an end. They attempted to rob a young woman in a rickshaw outside the crowded National Mosque at dagger point. She screamed and those nearby turned into a mob. Two of the muggers were brutally beaten to death and the third ended up in hospital in close proximity to Allah. A number of similar prior muggings had been reported in the area.

4/8/99

During hartal, I drafted a proposal for Nayeem to the US-based Media Development Loan Fund. I understand the Knight Foundation is a contributor to this fund. The text follows:

Media Development Loan Fund

Proposal for loan to launch a newspaper in Bangladesh

The Need

There is no truly independent daily newspaper in Bangladesh. All those that do exist serve government or corporate interests, or individual political aspirations. The newspaper we propose, the Bangla-language Natun Dhara (New Stream), would be an independent voice in the country and thus be different from all other print media.

The newspaper would be launched at a time when the fledgling nation is struggling to maintain a semblance of democracy. The country has many grave problems that range from extreme poverty, to a breakdown in law and order, to widespread corruption, to enormous health and education concerns. Against this dire background a number of Non-Governmental Organizations (NGOs) are striving to remedy these ills.

The Natun Dhara will have an editorial department exclusively devoted to investigative reporting. This department will be engaged full time in investigating issues concerning the public welfare. No other Bangladeshi newspaper has such a department.

How the Paper will Differ from Others

In addition to the differences mentioned above, the Natun Dhara will differ from other print media in Bangladesh in the following ways:

• Innovation in ownership. The paper will be jointly owned by entrepreneurs, readers, and staff members. Each will own a 33 1/3 percent share and have representation on a governing Board of Directors. Such a management structure is unknown in Bangladesh.

• The Editor and Publisher of Natun Dhara will be Nayeemul Islam Khan who has successfully launched three newspapers in the past, two dailies, and one weekly. He will pick a staff of highly trained professionals from a resource pool he has been cultivating for the last nine years as Executive Director of a small NGO, the Bangladesh Centre for Development, Journalism and Communication (BCDJC). Half the staff of approximately 150 persons will be women. Less than 10 percent of the staff on existing daily newspapers employ women.

• In addition, in-house training to maintain the highest ethical and skill standards will be conducted on a regular basis. No other paper in Bangladesh does this. It is thus hoped the paper will serve as a model for other journalists to emulate.

• A number of different editorial approaches are being considered. For example, most Bangla papers devote a considerable amount of space to sports coverage, in some cases four or more pages daily out of an average 16-page edition. It is felt that sports is one area that could be scaled back to accommodate longer, more significant investigative pieces on say, education, health, or other social issues.

• Another planned innovation is a four-page English-language section to appear as a weekly supplement within the primarily Bangla-language newspaper. The English section would carry articles different from those appearing elsewhere in the paper.

• The full-color paper, which will run on average 16 pages daily, will have a broad-sheet format, but will be narrower in size than those now in the market. Thus, it will be distinctive in both look and design. It will be completely formatted by computer and cost 6 taka per copy.

The Loan

Natun Dhara requires a loan for start-up purposes in the range of $450,000 to $600,000 to be paid back within five years. Some capital has already been pledged by local entrepreneurs. Other capital will be raised through reader participation and through employee contributions to be deducted from their salaries.

It is hoped that a strong paid subscriber base can be developed shortly after launch. Few, if any, Bangladeshi newspapers have developed a strong paid subscriber base, but links, such as with NGO activity centers, will be explored to establish such a base. The bulk of subscribers though will come from the ranks of doctors, lawyers, educators, and other professionals. A 30,000 circulation base is needed to make the paper financially viable. A detailed five-year financial forecast is presently being prepared to supplement this proposal.

Timeline

The newspaper would be launched early in 2001 after a pre-publication trial period of at least two months. At the moment, there are by latest count 284 dailies in the country with a total circulation of about 2.2 million. The total population of Bangladesh is about 126 million at present and is forecast to reach nearly 200 million by 2020.

Support

BCDJC will act as a primary support base for the new newspaper. It will provide training and training facilities for the paper's staff, a full research electronically accessed library, and clipping and filing services. In addition, it will make available its vast bank of contacts to the top editors and promising reporters. These include contacts within the media itself, within the government, within industry, within non-government organizations, within opposition parties, and within the general society as a whole.

Editorial Policy Summary

The newspaper will uphold the principles of independence, democracy, human rights and freedom of expression, with special attention to women, religious and ethnic minorities and the underprivileged of Bangladeshi society. Responsible journalism will act as an important catalyst in this regard. In order to check against any further erosion of the political culture, and to steer the nation toward democracy, albeit a Herculean task, the creation of a sane tradition of responsible journalism is an imperative. The Natun Dhara will relentlessly strive toward that end.

For further information on BCDJC and proposed newspaper see attached materials.

✳　✳　✳

During a light moment in an otherwise heavy discussion between Nayeem, the Army intelligence agent who works for *The Financial Express*, and myself about how reporters should cover military affairs, I innocently asked how I would get to the airport if a hartal were called on my departure date, August 15.

Nayeem solemnly responded: "No problem. By rickshaw. We will arrange a convoy of four. One will take you, another your baggage, and the lead one will carry Mukur, armed, of course. Azfar will bring up the rear. He, too, will be armed."

*   *   *

Tomorrow I have two social engagements. Rupa, my language teacher and her family, are taking me to lunch at the Sheraton. Then, Nayeem has invited me to dinner because his wife Monti is leaving the next day to return to her studies at Chittagong University.

The late sultry evening will be devoted to the Mango Tango. I have perfected my dip.

5/8/99

Nayeem is in seventh Muslim heaven! Several of his prayers have been answered. The Swedish Embassy informed him today that its government had approved his $200,000 bid for a journalism project that would bring training to 12 towns in rural Bangladesh, retroactive to August 1. The money will be spread over three years and assures his Centre of a livelihood over the period covered. Actually, funding was sought for a six-year period, but Sweden only funds projects for three years at a time. It is likely the grant will be extended.

In addition, the UNDP informed him that it would allow him to revise his bid on handling all media arrangements for its Asian Peace Conference the first week in September. Nayeem was really impressed with me because I had forecast, after figuring what was required, to the dollar what they were willing to spend—$20,000. He had over-ruled my calculations and bid $34,000. It seems the UNDP really wants him to handle the job and he agreed to revise his bid to fit within their budget.

Then, Nayeem has apparently worked out his differences with the Thomson Foundation. The Thomson people will be renting office space at the new School of Communications, which will help cover the Villa's rent. The Centre also will be helping with the Thomson project to raise the plight of children at the grassroots level. I believe a substantial sum is involved.

Finally, enquiring minds would like to know if Nayeem's first wife, now in exile in Sweden for her anti-Islamic Fundamentalist views, played any role in the Swedish government's decision to extend a grant to BCDJC.

A long day. Up at 5:30 am. Back at my Guest House at 11:30 pm.

Tomorrow is the last day of my Basic Journalism Course.

6/8/99

Nayeem's wife may not get to Chittagong. A BNP party leader was stabbed to death yesterday there shortly after midnight near his home and then his followers took to the streets damaging more than 100 vehicles, ripping up railroad tracks, and barricading all roads into and out of the port city. Paralysis ensued. The opposition blames Awami League activists, but the police say the murder may be related to a family feud over land. In addition, students at Chittagong University where Monti is studying shut down the university today with a series of protests over the administration's decision to suspend campus bus service.

* * *

The last day of my Basic Journalism Course went off without a hitch.
You know it's hot and humid when the Bangladeshis start gathering
around the air conditioner.

7/8/99

Nayeem let slip an interesting detail about his past today. His first job
as a reporter was for an Islamic Fundamentalist daily, the *Inqilar*, now
the third largest paper in the country. By all accounts, Nayeem was a
"radical" in those days. This might bear on the "floating" nature of his
politics, the staffing of the Centre, and some of Nayeem's close associates. The Islamic fundamentalist party Jamaat-I-Islam, which has its
own mouthpiece, the daily *Sangram*, became a coalition partner when
Khaleda Zia's BNP came to power in 1991 and is still a partner in the
current opposition which formed when Khaleda left office in 1996.
Nayeem, I believe, is a Sunni, as opposed to a Shiite, as are most
Bangladeshis. Shiites are fewer in number here but generally more
militant. At one time Nayeem may have flirted with the idea of becoming an Islamic fundamentalist, but such allegiance requires the rejection of all Western influences and values. Certainly, Nayeem does not
show any signs of doing that.

* * *

Nayeem decided today to scale back his request for a loan from the
Media Development Loan Fund to $450,000 to $600,000 from a million dollars. He has recalculated his needs and figures he can operate
initially without buying printing presses and some other equipment.

*   *   *

Well, well. Them bones, them bones, them dry bones. Now here's the worry of the Lord. Construction workers have dug up skulls, teeth and bones from what appears to be a mass grave left from Bangladesh's 1971 war for Jindependence. The skulls and some of the bones bore markings from bullets or meat cleavers, according to Akku Chowdhury, a spokesman for the Liberation War Museum. Nearly 3 million Bangladeshis were killed during the nine-month war that won Bangladesh's (East Pakistan's) independence from Pakistan.

Digging began last month at the Noori Mosque in Dhaka's Mirpur district. Since then, more than 500 pieces of bone, five skulls, two sets of teeth and several shoes have turned up. At least 62 bone fragments were turned up this week.The remains were found in an abandoned well closed in 1971.

8/8/99

Police yesterday bulldozed thousands of make-shift homes in two Dhaka slum areas, leaving an estimated 20,000 or so people homeless. The action occurred two days after a police officer patrolling in one of the slum areas was shot and killed by unidentified gunmen. Two other police officers were wounded during the attack. Police officials contend the slums house many robbers, thieves, and other criminals. At least two and a half million of Dhaka's more than nine million people live in slum conditions.

Police also demolished nearly 500 small grocery and vegetable shops in the area.

Many of the new homeless sought shelter on the streets.

9-11/8/99

The first day of my Workshop on the Sundarbans passed without incident. There were 13 participants and no one was eaten by a Royal Bengal Tiger. Only one participant was a woman and her apartment was robbed on the second day. It seems the woman who shared the flat took off with a good many of the participant's possessions. Judging from evaluation forms and direct feedback, the workshop was a success. The participants were mostly senior reporters for newspapers and one worked for a wire service.

One participant, however, was a young freelancer for *The New Nation*, Mohammad Arifur Rahman, who sought my help in trying to get to America where he wants to take up doctoral studies in political science—specifically, bilateral relations between Bangladesh and the United States. His was a sad tale. He needs a regular paying job because he wants to marry a girl from his hometown of Jessore, but is a poor lad presently living off the kindness of his elder brother. A few months back, he was covering university campus affairs, but, because he tried to write about campus ills, his life was threatened by student goons (verified by the Committee to Protect Journalists in New York) and he was forced to give up the education beat.

The university campuses in Bangladesh are festering cesspools. On the last day of the workshop, a gunbattle erupted between two student factions of the ruling Awami League on the Chittagong University campus. Twenty of the student activists were wounded, two critically.

And at Dhaka University recently, one student held a large party for his friends to celebrate his 100th rape. Incredible! There are two notorious student groups on the Dhaka campus—one known as the

Rapists and the other the Murderers. This is the appalling atmosphere in which higher education is conducted in Bangladesh. Welcome to Guns, Drugs, and Rape 101. It seems the faculty and administration are in as much fear of these terrorists as the students and police.

12/8/99

Gun-battles of more than an hour's duration continued for a second straight day today on Chittagong University's campus, forcing the closure of the state institution indefinitely. Some 50 individuals were wounded, including four police officers, two of whom were in critical condition. The gun-battles were again between two factions of the student wing of the ruling Awami League. The student activists were protesting a university administration decision to suspend campus bus transportation.

* * *

Thousands of Bangladeshi slum dwellers clashed with police today over a government drive to oust them from their homes. The police fired teargas to clear nearly 4,000 people who were blocking the Dhaka-Aricha highway to protest recent government evictions. About 50 people were reported injured and more than 30 were arrested after the protesters from the city's Shamoli area threw stones at police trying to disperse them. The protesters damaged at least 100 vehicles in the area and brought traffic to a standstill for several hours.

Authorities have evicted about 20,000 people in the last five days from different Dhaka slum areas, home to about two and a half million people of the city's more than nine million total.

The High Court on Wednesday ordered a suspension of the evictions until August 19 on a petition that argues the government has been evicting people without prior notice.

But police apparently intend to continue the evictions in an effort to gain revenge for recent killings of police officers and to curb rising crime in general in the city.

Home Ministry officials said the government had already taken steps to rehabilitate evicted slum dwellers and that those who left voluntarily would be rehoused.

The Bangladesh Krishi (agriculture) Bank has reportedly pledged to finance an $825 million five-year government plan to resettle some four million slum dwellers in Dhaka and other cities.

13/8/99

The monsoon season has returned. A day of rain, packing, and prayer. Played two games of chess with Azfar who came to collect the books and other items I'm leaving behind—won one, lost one.

14/8/99

A going away party for me is planned at the Centre, beginning at 5:30 pm. My Bangla teacher Rupa has organized a cultural evening. Participants from my most recent Basic Journalism Workshop will be on hand to collect their certificates and wish me well. Nayeem is big on ceremonies. The Centre has bought me a number of small gifts as a token of their appreciation for my services. It is unlikely they will fit in my already overcrowded suitcases.

I have prepared a "tear," to add to my collection.

On Leaving Dhaka

I leave on the very morrow
silver wings will carry me thus
From the Bay of Bengal
and its mighty tigers
To Galway Bay and the IRA

Yes, Will,
parting is such sweet sorrow
Six months is but a sparrow.
Too little a time
for a rickshaw ride
to democracy's rhyme
in prime hartal time

I'll cry a new river for you Bangladesh.
You will overflow my
muddied memory embankments.
You cannot evict me
from your heart Bangladesh.

Today is also a day for settling final bills, developing film, a run to FedEx, and a beard trim and hair cut. I think I still have one hair left.

*   *   *

Ten have died in a mudslide in Chittagong and thousands are marooned in the wake of flash floods in that area. The university there has been closed indefinitely as a result of the gun-battles on campus.

15/8/99

Yet another national holiday. This time a National Day of Mourning for Bangabandhu or Sheikh Myibur Rahman, first President of Bangladesh, assassinated in 1975 by army officers during a coup. Loudspeakers all over town have been carrying an edited version of one of his more firebrand speeches.

My plane departs at 9:10 pm and I plan to be on it.

Epilogue

Village water pump, a source of life and death.

ow, back in the United States and mulling over my experience in Bangladesh, I'm left with a sense of rot and decay, hopelessness and despair. I'm left begging for a solution. Political infighting, violence, corruption, and the ravages of extreme poverty are combining to scuttle all hope there. I ask myself do I really believe that a civil war could be at hand in Bangladesh? The answer is yes.

Since my departure another opposition-led strike—and there will be many more— has closed banks, transport, ports and factories across the country. Each such one-day strike costs Bangladesh roughly $50 million in lost revenue and exports, a big drain for a country with annual per capita income of only $289.

Annual investment in Bangladesh is currently estimated at about 12 percent of Gross Domestic Product (GDP) against a requirement of about 25 percent to make any visible impact on employment and growth.

Bangladesh's economy grew by 5.2 percent in 1998-99 (July-June) compared to 5.6 in the previous year. GDP growth in 1999-2000 has been targeted at 7 percent, which would be possible only if the country attained political stability allowing uninterrupted production.

About half the population of 126 million still live in poverty while unemployment has shown no sign of easing. Of the total population, some 30 million people are classified as "ultra poor," which translates to about one or two meals a week per person and a lot of extended stomachs.

Shortly after my departure, the World Bank informed Bangladesh that it would offer aid of only $310 million in fiscal 1999/2000 (July-June) against a commitment of $653 million in the previous year. The bank had committed a total of more than $1 billion, including flood-related assistance worth $368 million, in fiscal 1998/99. But World Bank officials said the bank would propose a reduced amount of $310 million for the current year in view of the country's lack of progress in reforms. Other donors have indicated their kindnesses may have limits.

In re-reading my journal fragments, I realized something was missing. A sense of *deja vu*. Like the flooding, it has all happened before— the street violence, the plots, the lapses in law and order, the police combing operations, the training efforts—all of it. I present it here with a newcomer's awe and incredulity as if it were happening for the first time. But this, I now realize, is the accepted Bangladeshi way of life from which there is no obvious way out. What did I discover on my Knight quest? Bangladesh is not a Democracy, but a Mastanocracy, a society at the mercy of the armed individual.

On the surface, the waters are deceptively placid with sufferance, but the undercurrents in Bangladesh—roiled by power, greed, and avarice—are sufficiently treacherous to drown out the prayers of the predominantly Muslim populous for divine intervention, and suck the drowning Bangladeshi into civil war, perhaps within three to five years. Such a conflict will involve nuclear-capable India and Pakistan, still clashing militarily at this writing over Kashmir, and will likely solve few of Bangladesh's problems. Although it may bring some necessary change, the cost will be great, and the waters will run red with the blood of a good many Bangla poets.

President Clinton's decision to visit India, Bangladesh and Pakistan—the three principal countries of South Asia in late March of 2000— is fraught with political risk and danger. Together these countries are home to one out of every five people in the world. The future of these countries will affect the course of the post-Cold War world and the status of major US interests. The trip—the first by an American president to India in twenty-two years, to Pakistan in thirty,

and the first ever to Bangladesh—provides an opportunity to provide a rounded picture of a part of the world that is foreign to most Americans.

South Asia today is a far more dangerous place than it was only one or two years ago. In particular, the deterioration of the internal situation in Pakistan and the relationship between Pakistan and India, which I have outlined in this book, sharply limits what the President can hope to accomplish during his journey.

As this journal attests, the President will step into a clouded and dangerous political picture in Bangladesh. The government and other important segments of the population are at constant loggerheads. The visit thus is a chance to educate Americans about the significance of South Asia while sending selected messages to the governments and peoples of the region.

Paul Ryder Ryan
Plainfield, MA
December 30, 1999

PHOTO CREDITS: The photographers who took the pictures appearing in this book shall remain anonymous. During the author's stay in Bangladesh, more than 13 photojournalists were seriously injured, many by policemen, while doing their jobs.

Munewata Press. P.O. Box 130, Cummington, MA 01026
www.booksonasia.com

MUNEWATA PRESS

ORDER FORM

Check Choice and indicate number of books

_____ Bangladesh 2000: On the Brink of Civil War
by Paul Ryder Ryan
$13.95 Paperback. ISBN 0-9662707-6-2

_____ Khmer Rouge End Game
by Paul Ryder Ryan
$16.95 Paperback. ISBN 0-9662707-4-6

_____ China Daily: Between the Lines
by Paul Ryder Ryan
$21.95 Paperback. ISBN 0-9662707-3-8

Please add $3.20 to cover shipping and handling.

Make checks or money orders payable to: **Munewata Press**

Name _____

Address_____

City_____ State_____ Zip _____

Please allow 4-6 weeks for delivery.

Munewata Press. P.O. Box 130, Cummington, MA 01026
www.booksonasia.com